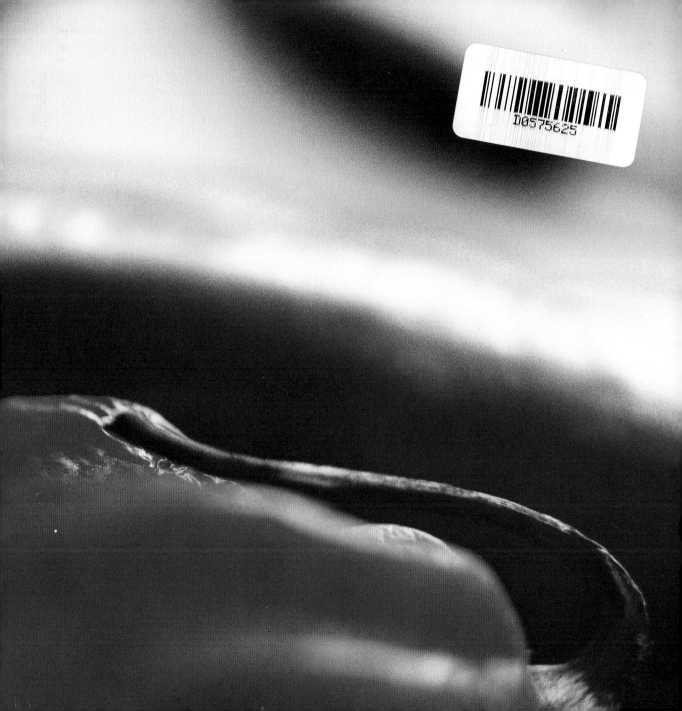

easy hot & spicy

easy hot & spicy

favorite fiery dishes from around the world

RYLAND
PETERS
& SMALL

LONDON NEW YORK

First published in the United States in 2008
by Ryland Peters & Small
519 Broadway, 5th Floor
New York, NY 10012
www.rylandpeters.com

10 9 8 7 6 5 4 3 2

Printed and bound in China

Library of Congress Cataloging-in-Publication Data

Easy hot & spicy: favorite fiery dishes from around the world / [text, Ghillie Basan ... et al.]. -- 1st U.S. ed.
    p. cm.
  Includes index.
  ISBN 978-1-84597-632-3
  1. Cookery (Spices) 2. Cookery, International. I. Basan, Ghillie. II. Title: Easy hot and spicy.
  TX819.A1E35 2008
  641.6'383--dc22
                                2007045274

Senior Designer Paul Tilby
Senior Editors Julia Charles, Clare Double
Picture Research Emily Westlake
Production Gemma John, Paul Harding
Art Director Leslie Harrington
Publishing Director Alison Starling

NOTES:

All spoon measurements are level unless otherwise specified.

Ovens should be preheated to the specified temperature. If using a convection oven, cooking times should be reduced according to the manufacturer's instructions.

Uncooked or partly cooked eggs should not be served to the very young, the very old or frail, or to pregnant women.

Specialty Asian ingredients are available in larger supermarkets and Asian stores.

To sterilize preserving jars, wash them in hot, soapy water and rinse in boiling water. Place in a large saucepan and then cover with hot water. With the saucepan lid on, bring the water to a boil and continue boiling for 15 minutes. Turn off the heat, then leave the jars in the hot water until just before they are to be filled. Sterilize the lids for 5 minutes, by boiling, or according to the manufacturer's instructions. Jars should be filled and sealed while they are still hot.

contents

feel the burn...

Whether you fancy a curry with a kick or an exotically spiced tagine, you're sure to find something perfect here. These quick and easy recipes have been specially chosen to help even the busiest people enjoy delicious, fresh, home-cooked food.

Hot and spicy dishes are so much more than one element, and they vary in flavor as much as they do in color. An incredible variety of chiles and herbs and spices is used to create the tastebud-tingling flavors that you find in fiery food from around the globe. India, Thailand, China, North Africa, Mexico, South America, and Spain are just some of the countries and regions represented here, and all of them have a tradition of tasty, spicy food—the very best of which you'll find in this recipe collection.

Included are great ideas for deliciously different party nibbles and food for sharing plus simple recipes for appetizers and light lunches. For the health conscious, fish and seafood dishes make a good choice, as they are light on calories but big on taste. Meat eaters will enjoy the more substantial dishes, from delicious beef curries to a slow-cooked tagine— perfect for a cosy night in. Chicken dishes are great for everyday eating throughout the year, from a warming Thai curry to something spicy cooked on the grill in summer. Food for vegetarians is also brought to life with the addition of heat—try one of the spicy Mexican bean dishes or a crisp Chinese stir-fry.

So why not turn up the heat in your kitchen and discover how exciting sizzling hot and aromatic food from around the world can be.

small bites and dips

1 lb. uncooked, shelled and deveined shrimp

4 kaffir lime leaves, very finely chopped, or grated zest of 1 lime

4 scallions, finely chopped

2 tablespoons chopped cilantro

1 egg

1 tablespoon Thai fish sauce

⅓ cup rice flour or cornstarch

peanut or safflower oil, for frying

chili jam

1 lb. ripe tomatoes, coarsely chopped

3–4 red chiles, coarsely chopped

2 garlic cloves, chopped

1 teaspoon grated fresh ginger

2 tablespoons light soy sauce

1¼ cups palm sugar or brown sugar

½ cup white wine vinegar

½ teaspoon sea salt

*2 preserving jars, about
1 cup each, sterilized*

serves 6 (makes 24 cakes)

Thai fish, shrimp, or crab cakes are quick and easy to make—perfect as a first course or as a spicy snack with drinks. If you have time, marinate the shrimp mixture for 30 minutes or so. To make this recipe simpler, you can use a prepared chili sauce.

thai shrimp cakes
with chili jam

To make the chili jam, put the tomatoes, chiles, and garlic in a food processor and purée until smooth. Transfer to a saucepan, add the ginger, soy sauce, sugar, vinegar, and salt, and bring to a boil. Cook for 30–35 minutes, stirring occasionally until thick and glossy.

Warm the jars in a low oven, pour in the thickened jam, and let cool completely. Seal and store in the refrigerator.

To make the shrimp cakes, put the shrimp into a food processor and blend to a purée. Add the lime leaves, scallions, cilantro, egg, fish sauce, and rice flour, blend briefly, and transfer to a bowl. Using damp hands, shape the mixture into 24 patties, 2 inches diameter.

Pour ½-inch depth of the oil in a skillet, heat for 1 minute over medium heat, then add the cakes, spaced apart. Sauté in batches for 2 minutes on each side until golden brown. Remove, drain on paper towels and keep them warm in a low oven while you cook the remainder. Serve with chili jam or sweet chili sauce.

Shrimp makes the fastest, most impressive dish you can imagine. If you want to use precooked shrimp, just sprinkle them with the chili oil and lemon juice and serve with the cool and refreshing pesto.

shrimp with chili oil
and pistachio and mint pesto

To make the pesto, put the pistachios, mint, garlic, and scallions in a food processor and grind coarsely. Add the oil and purée until fairly smooth and green. Stir in the vinegar and season to taste. Set aside while you prepare the shrimp, or store in the refrigerator for up to 5 days.

Put the shrimp in a shallow dish and sprinkle with the chili oil, salt, and pepper. Cover and let marinate for at least 30 minutes or longer, if possible.

When ready to serve, thread the shrimp onto skewers and cook on a preheated outdoor grill or stove-top grill pan, or under a hot broiler, for about 2 minutes on each side until charred and tender—the flesh should be just opaque. Do not overcook or the shrimp will be tough.

Put on separate plates or a large platter, sprinkle with fresh lemon juice, and serve with the pesto and crusty bread to mop up the juices.

24 large uncooked shrimp, shelled and deveined

¼ cup chili oil

freshly squeezed juice of 1 lemon

pistachio and mint pesto

2 oz. shelled pistachios, about ⅓ cup

a bunch of mint

1 garlic clove, crushed

2 scallions, chopped

½ cup extra virgin olive oil

1 tablespoon white wine vinegar

sea salt and freshly ground black pepper

skewers

serves 4

2 spicy chorizo sausages

20 freshly shucked oysters

shallot vinegar

3 tablespoons red wine vinegar

2 tablespoons finely chopped shallot

1 tablespoon chopped chives

sea salt and freshly ground black pepper

toothpicks

a large platter filled with ice cubes

serves 4

This combination may sound slightly unusual, but it is totally delicious. Fresh oyster, a nibble of hot sausage, and a sip of chilled dry white wine is a taste sensation —try it, you'll be amazed.

oysters with spicy chorizo

To make the shallot vinegar, put the ingredients in a bowl and mix well. Pour into a small dish and set aside until required.

Preheat the broiler, then cook the sausages for 8–10 minutes or until cooked through. Cut the sausages into bite-size pieces and spike them onto toothpicks. Arrange in a small dish. Put the oysters on their half shells and arrange on top of the ice. Serve with the chorizo and shallot vinegar.

These little fried cakes of potato and chorizo with a crisp corn salsa are based on a Mexican dish using queso fresco, a mild fresh cheese. This recipe substitutes fresh goat cheese, which has an affinity with spicy food though it isn't traditional. You could also use feta cheese, as long as it's not too salty.

tortitas de papa
with chorizo
and corn salsa verde

Put the potatoes in a large saucepan, bring to a boil, then simmer for 15 to 20 minutes or until tender. Drain well and, when cool enough to handle, peel and pass through a potato ricer, food mill, or a sieve into a large bowl.

Heat a non-stick skillet, add the chorizo, and sauté gently for 5 to 10 minutes until the fat renders. Lift out the chorizo with a slotted spoon, let it cool slightly, then add to the bowl of potato. Add the garlic, scallions, and goat cheese and mix. Add the egg, salt, and pepper and mix well.

Divide the mixture into 18 parts and form into small flat cakes. Roll each potato cake in the breadcrumbs, pressing gently so the crumbs stick. Set aside while you make the salsa.

To make the salsa verde, put the mustard in a small bowl and beat in the lime juice or wine vinegar. Continue beating, adding the olive oil in a thin stream until amalgamated. Stir in the remaining ingredients, then add salt and pepper to taste.

Heat a thin layer of oil in a large skillet and sauté the potato cakes in batches until golden brown all over (about 8 to 10 minutes). Drain on paper towels and keep them warm while you cook the remaining potato cakes.

Serve with the salsa and a crisp salad.

1½ lb. potatoes, unpeeled, scrubbed well

3 chorizo sausages, peeled and crumbled

1 garlic clove, crushed

4 scallions, chopped

8 oz. goat cheese, crumbled

1 large egg, beaten

½ cup fine dry breadcrumbs

olive oil, for cooking

salt and freshly ground black pepper

corn salsa verde

1 tablespoon Dijon mustard

1 tablespoon freshly squeezed lime juice or wine vinegar

⅔ cup extra-virgin olive oil

2 tablespoons capers, rinsed and chopped

½ cup canned corn kernels, drained

2 scallions, finely chopped

1–2 garlic cloves, very finely chopped

6 tablespoons chopped flat leaf parsley

6 tablespoons chopped cilantro

1–2 green chiles, finely chopped

salt and freshly ground black pepper

serves 6 (makes 18)

1½ lb. large floury potatoes, peeled

2 green chiles

½ teaspoon crushed dried red chiles

1 small onion, finely chopped

1 teaspoon salt

1 teaspoon ground cumin

1 teaspoon ground turmeric

2 tablespoons chopped cilantro leaves

2 tablespoons unsalted butter, melted

1 cup all-purpose flour

vegetable oil, for frying

coconut and mint chutney

1½ cups grated fresh coconut or ⅔ cup unsweetened desiccated coconut

1 cup plain yogurt

1 green chile, seeded and chopped

2 tablespoons chopped mint

½ teaspoon salt

½ teaspoon sugar

serves 8–10 (makes 64)

India has dozens of different kinds of bread—plain, flavored with spices as here, or with spicy fillings. They are served with curry or dhal, but these roti are made smaller to eat as a snack. You could continue the potato theme and serve roti with vodka-based drinks—vodka is sometimes made from potatoes, as well as from grains.

mini potato roti with coconut and mint chutney

If using desiccated coconut to make the chutney, place in a bowl and cover with warm water. Let soak for about 20 minutes, then strain through a sieve, pressing the coconut against the sieve to squeeze out any excess moisture.

Combine all the chutney ingredients in a bowl, mix well, and set aside.

Cook the potatoes in boiling salted water, drain, and mash well. Seed and finely chop the green chiles. Add to the potatoes and stir in all the remaining ingredients, except the flour. Gradually mix in the flour until you have a soft dough. Divide the dough into 64 equal pieces. Taking one piece at a time, roll out on a floured board to a 3-inch circle. Continue with the remaining pieces.

Brush a heavy-based skillet with oil and, when hot, cook the roti 2 or 3 at a time for 1 to 2 minutes on each side until lightly browned. Keep warm in a low oven while you cook the remainder. Serve with the coconut and mint chutney.

¼ teaspoon pasilla chili flakes, with seeds

1 dried chipotle chile, seeded and chopped

6 thick slices jalapeño in brine or 1 large fresh jalapeño, seeded

about 5 large cabbage leaves, trimmed of tough stalks

1 small onion

1 tablespoon chopped oregano or marjoram

3 tablespoons white wine vinegar

3 tablespoons rice vinegar

⅓ cup pineapple juice

sea salt, to taste

serves 6 as a relish

This crunchy relish from Mexico is made with three chile varieties, revealing their individual flavors—licorice-like pasilla chili flakes, smoky chipotle chiles, and jalapeño slices—but you could use just the jalapeño and one other.

chilito

Soak the dried pasilla and chipotle chiles in 2 teaspoons warm water for about 15 minutes, then drain. Finely chop the jalapeños. Set aside.

Finely shred the cabbage in a food processor and transfer to a bowl. Repeat with the onion and add to the bowl. Add the oregano, chiles, and salt and toss well.

Mix the vinegars and juice in a small bowl and add to the bowl. Mix very well (the liquid is just enough to coat the vegetables—it is not meant to submerge them). Set aside for 1–2 hours to develop the flavors. Serve a little chilito on the side with Mexican entrée dishes, burritos, or corn chips, and other condiments.

This sauce or condiment is always on hand in Mexico. Add it to anything you think needs a bit of livening up, or serve with corn chips and margaritas or Bloody Marys.

salsa roja

Break the chiles in half and shake out the seeds. Heat the oil in a skillet, add the chiles and sauté until they turn bright red. Remove with a slotted spoon and put into a bowl. Cover with water and let soak for about 30 minutes.

Add the garlic to the pan and sauté until golden. Transfer to a food processor, add the drained chiles, and chop coarsely. Add the oregano and tomatoes and chop again. Add salt and pepper to taste and serve with corn chips.

12 dried New Mexico chiles

½ cup safflower oil

3 garlic cloves, halved

1 tablespoon chopped oregano

6 large, ripe tomatoes, skinned and seeded

sea salt and freshly ground black pepper

corn chips, to serve

makes about 2 cups

Vietnam is known for its delicate cuisine. It is notable for its great use of herbs, while spices, when used, are balanced and often gentle. Typical in southern cooking are spices such as ginger, galangal, star anise, tamarind, chiles, and occasionally turmeric, five-spice powder, and curry powder. This appetizing starter of stuffed baby squid, spiced with star anise, ginger, and pepper, is a fine example. Nuóc cham is the traditional Vietnamese dipping sauce, but you could also use soy sauce or chili sauce.

vietnamese spiced squid

To make the dipping sauce, use a mortar and pestle to grind the garlic, chile, and sugar to form a paste. Stir in the lime juice, fish sauce, and about 3 tablespoons water. Transfer to a dipping bowl.

To prepare the stuffing, pour boiling water over the noodles and let soak for 4 minutes or according to the instructions on the package. Drain well, coarsely chop the noodles, and transfer to a large bowl.

Put 1 tablespoon of the peanut oil into a wok, heat well, swirl to coat, then add the scallions, ginger, and garlic. Stir-fry for a few minutes until softened, then add to the noodle bowl. Chop the squid tentacles and add to the ingredients in the bowl. Add the pork, star anise, fish sauce, sugar, salt, and ¼ teaspoon of cracked black pepper, and mix well.

Stuff the squid bodies, leaving a little space at the top. Secure closed with toothpicks.

Heat the remaining oil in a skillet and add the squid. Cook gently for 10–12 minutes, until lightly browned in places and cooked through.

Slice the squid or leave them whole. Serve with fresh herbs and the nuóc cham.

*Note To prepare the squid, cut off the tentacles and chop them coarsely. Cut off and discard the eye sections. Rinse out the bodies, discarding the tiny transparent quill. If you can't find squid with tentacles, buy an extra body, chop it coarsely, then add to the stuffing mixture.

1 oz. cellophane rice noodles (rice vermicelli), about 1 small bundle

½ cup peanut oil

3 scallions, chopped

1 inch fresh ginger, peeled and grated

2 garlic cloves, chopped

16 prepared, cleaned baby squid with tentacles reserved*

12 oz. ground pork

2–3 "petals" of 1 star anise, finely crushed (about ¼ teaspoon ground)

1 tablespoon Thai fish sauce

a pinch of sugar

sea salt and cracked black pepper

a handful of mixed Asian herbs, to serve

nuóc cham dipping sauce

1 garlic clove, crushed

1 red bird's eye chile, finely sliced

2 tablespoons sugar

freshly squeezed juice of ½ lime

¼ cup Thai fish sauce

toothpicks

makes 16

1 cup Chinese glutinous rice or Japanese sushi rice*

1 teaspoon salt

1 teaspoon sugar

2 teaspoons white rice vinegar

½ cup firm tofu

1 garlic clove, crushed

1 inch fresh ginger, peeled and grated

2 tablespoons light soy sauce

2 tablespoons sweet chili sauce

2 tablespoons peanut oil

6 eggs, beaten

6 asparagus spears or 12 green beans, cooked

3 scallions, halved lengthwise

soy sauce mixed with a little grated ginger root, to serve

makes 24

Glutinous rice is sold in Asian foodstores. If unavailable, sushi rice can be used—or even short-grain rice.

Egg fried rice is a popular Chinese dish and Japanese sushi makes excellent party food. This recipe mixes the two together. Make these rolls in the morning and keep them chilled until 30 minutes before serving.

egg rolls with chili tofu

Pour 2 cups water into a medium saucepan, bring to a boil, then add the rice and salt. Reduce the heat to a low simmer, cover and cook for 12 minutes without lifting the lid. Remove from the heat and let stand for 5 minutes. Put the sugar and vinegar in a small bowl or cup, stir to dissolve, then mix into the rice. Let cool.

Cut the tofu into ⅛-inch slices. Arrange in a single layer in a flat dish. Put the garlic, ginger, soy, and sweet chili sauce in a small pitcher, mix well, then pour over the tofu. Set aside for 10 minutes.

Heat 1 tablespoon of the oil in a large skillet, add the tofu, and cook for 1½ minutes on each side. Remove from the pan, cut the slices into ⅛-inch strips, then set aside.

Heat 1 teaspoon of the remaining oil in the same skillet and add one-third of the beaten egg. Swirl the egg around to cover the base of the skillet and cook for 2 minutes until set. Carefully remove the omelet to a plate and cook the remaining egg mixture in the same way in 2 more batches.

Stretch a piece of plastic wrap (about 4 inches longer than your omelet) on a flat surface and put 1 omelet in the middle. Spread with one-third of the rice. Close to the near edge, arrange a line of tofu, asparagus or beans, and scallions—use one-third of the ingredients for each roll. Carefully roll up the omelet, pulling away the plastic as you go. Wrap in the plastic until ready to serve.

Unwrap the rolls and slice into 1-inch pieces. Serve with the soy sauce.

You can use either fresh squid or frozen, whole or cleaned,
for this—though if they're cleaned, they won't have their
pretty flowerlike tentacles. Squid is equally good, if not
better, after being frozen—freezing serves the same
purpose as the fisherman beating the fish against a stone
to tenderize it.

spicy crumbed squid strips

If using fresh squid, you will need to clean it first. Pull the tentacles out of the body, then cut off the rosette of tentacles—you may need to press out the tiny hard piece from the middle of the rosette. Keep the tentacles and bodies and discard the rest. Pull the quill (the transparent "spine") out of the body and discard it. You can remove the thin purplish skin if you like, but it is edible. Rinse the bodies, pat dry, and cut lengthwise into 4–6 strips.

Put the breadcrumbs, garlic, ginger, parsley, chiles, five-spice, and salt in a bowl and mix well. Mix the egg and soy sauce in a second bowl.

Fill a wok or saucepan one-third full with the oil and heat to 350°F, or until a small cube of bread turns golden in 45 seconds. Dust the squid with flour, dip into the egg, then the breadcrumb mixture. Fry in batches of 8 for 2–3 minutes, then remove and drain on crumpled paper towels. Keep them warm while you cook the remainder.

Serve with sweet chili sauce.

6–8 medium (6–8 inches) squid, about 1 lb.

¾ cup fresh breadcrumbs

2 garlic cloves, crushed

1 inch fresh ginger, peeled and grated

a small bunch of parsley, finely chopped

2 red or green chiles, finely chopped

2 teaspoons five-spice powder

1 teaspoon salt

2 eggs, beaten

2 tablespoons soy sauce

peanut oil, for frying

flour, for dusting

sweet chili sauce, to serve

serves 4–6 (makes 32)

Chili beef makes a great filling for wontons, which are more traditionally filled with minced pork and shrimp. They can be fried in advance and reheated in the oven at 375°F for 8 minutes before serving.

crispy chili beef wontons

To make the filling, slice the steak into thin strips and, if they are wider than ½ inch, slice them in half lengthwise. Put in a bowl and mix in the sesame oil, vinegar, and oyster sauce.

Using a small food processor or mortar and pestle, grind the chiles, ginger, garlic, and salt to a coarse paste. Add to the steak, mix well, and set aside for about 30 minutes.

Put 1 tablespoon of filling in the center of each wonton wrapper, brush around the edges with the egg white, and gather up, twisting to seal.

Fill a wok or skillet one-third full with the oil and heat to 375°F or until a small cube of bread turns golden brown in 30 seconds. Cook the wontons in batches of 6 for 2–3 minutes until golden and crisp. Drain on paper towels, then serve with plum sauce.

1 lb. sirloin steak

1 tablespoon sesame oil

2 teaspoons white rice vinegar

3 tablespoons oyster sauce

2–4 red chiles, seeded and chopped

2 inches fresh ginger, peeled and chopped

3 garlic cloves

1 teaspoon salt

32 large wonton wrappers*

1 egg white, beaten

peanut oil, for frying

plum sauce, to serve

serves 4–6 (makes 32)

Packages vary, but contain about 40 large (4-inch) or 70 small (3-inch) wrappers. Leftovers can be frozen.

1 lb. ground pork

6 garlic cloves, crushed

2 stalks lemongrass, finely sliced

1 bunch cilantro, finely chopped

2 red chiles, cored and diced

1 tablespoon brown sugar

1 tablespoon Thai fish sauce

1 egg, beaten

salt and freshly ground black pepper

peanut oil, for frying

chili dipping sauce

½ cup white rice vinegar

2–6 small chiles or 1 large red chile, finely sliced

1 tablespoon Thai fish sauce

1 scallion, finely sliced (optional)

½–1 tablespoon brown sugar

serves 4

A delicious main course served with other Asian dishes, and also great at a drinks party. Use fat Fresno chiles for a mild flavor, or bird's eye chiles for blinding heat.

thai pork balls
with chili dipping sauce

Mix all the ingredients for the chili dipping sauce in a small bowl, stir to dissolve the sugar, then set aside to develop the flavors.

To make the pork balls, place all the remaining ingredients, except the peanut oil, in a bowl and mix well. Dip your hands in water, take about 1–2 tablespoons of the mixture, and roll it into a ball. Repeat with the remaining mixture.

Fill a wok one-third full of peanut oil and heat until a cube of bread browns in 30 seconds. Add the pork balls, 6 at a time, and deep-fry in batches until golden brown. Remove and drain on crumpled paper towels, keeping them warm in the oven until all the balls are done. Serve with the chili dipping sauce.

For this dish only the thick part of the chicken wings is used, marinated in a blend of lemongrass and chile. The crunchiness of the deep-fried lemongrass makes an interesting texture. The winglets are simple to prepare. Run a knife around the narrow end of the wing, just below the knuckle, then use your knife to cut and push the flesh down the bone to form a little ball at the bottom. The bone then acts as a handle, perfect for finger food.

3 stalks of lemongrass, finely chopped

2 small chiles, finely chopped

3 tablespoons oyster sauce

1 tablespoon Thai fish sauce

1 teaspoon sugar

1 lb. chicken winglets
(also known as drumettes)*

peanut or safflower oil, for deep-frying

sprigs of cilantro, to serve

sweet and hot sauce

4 tablespoons sugar

6 tablespoons rice vinegar

½ teaspoon salt

2 small red chiles, finely chopped

an electric deep-fryer (optional)

serves 4

chicken wings
with lemongrass and sweet and hot sauce

Put the lemongrass, chiles, oyster sauce, fish sauce, and sugar in a bowl and beat with a fork. Add the chicken winglets, turn to coat, and set aside to marinate for 15 minutes.

Meanwhile, make the sauce. Put the sugar, vinegar, and salt in a saucepan and heat, stirring, until the sugar dissolves. Add the chiles and 4 tablespoons water, stir well, and simmer until it becomes a thin syrup. Pour into a dipping bowl.

Fill a wok or deep-fryer one-third full with the oil or to the manufacturer's recommended level. Heat until a scrap of noodle will puff up immediately.

Working in batches if necessary, fry the chicken wings until golden brown. Remove with a slotted spoon, drain, and serve with sweet and hot sauce and sprigs of cilantro.

*Note If you are unable to find chicken winglets, buy the whole wings and cut off the last 2 joints. Use them for another recipe or to make stock.

Thai dips are mostly made from chiles. They are used both as dipping sauces and for spooning over rice or other dishes. This dip, as its name implies, is made from young, green, strongly flavored chiles and is wonderful to serve with drinks at parties. Seed the chiles if you like.

vegetables
with spicy Thai dip
of young chiles

Wrap the chiles, garlic, shallots, and tomatoes in foil and put under a preheated medium broiler. Cook until they begin to soften, turning once or twice. Unwrap, then pound with a mortar and pestle to form a liquid paste.

Add the lemon juice, soy sauce, salt, and sugar to the paste, stirring well, then spoon into a small dipping bowl.

Serve as a dipping sauce, surrounded by crisp salad ingredients, such as lettuce, cucumber, radish, and celery, or with raw or blanched vegetables.

4 large green chiles

4 small green chiles

6 large garlic cloves

6 pink Thai shallots or 3 regular ones

4 medium tomatoes

2 tablespoons freshly squeezed lime or lemon juice

2 tablespoons light soy sauce

½ teaspoon salt

2 teaspoons sugar

your choice of salad or other vegetables, to serve

serves 4

The name of this Greek dish, tyrohtipiti, means "beaten cheese." It originated in the beautiful city of Thessaloniki, but is fast becoming popular all over Greece. Its color varies according to the type of bell peppers used and the heat of the chiles. It can be pink or red; in Thessaloniki it is green, as is the version here.

feta and chile dip

2 hot green chiles

1 large red or green bell pepper

8 oz. feta cheese, thickly sliced

¼ cup extra virgin olive oil

freshly squeezed juice of 1 small lemon

3–4 tablespoons milk

1 teaspoon hot red chili flakes

1 tablespoon finely chopped
flat leaf parsley

freshly ground black pepper

toasted bread or crudités, to serve

a metal skewer

serves 6

Thread the chiles on a metal skewer and put over a low gas flame or on a preheated grill. Turn them over until scorched. Put the bell pepper over the flame and do the same until it feels soft and partially scorched. The pepper will take longer than the chiles. Set aside until cool enough to handle.

Seed and peel the bell pepper and do the same with the chiles, which will be a little more difficult. Wipe off any blackened bits with paper towels. (Beware of the hot chiles.)

Put the chiles, bell pepper, feta, olive oil, lemon juice, milk, and black pepper in a food processor and blend until creamy. If the mixture is too stiff, add a little more milk. Remove to a plate or bowl, sprinkle the chili flakes and parsley on top and chill lightly. Serve with toast or crudités.

This spicy Middle Eastern chickpea dip is good served simply with grilled pita bread or with spicy kabobs or garlicky broiled poussin. It is always present among the exotic array of dishes on meze tables everywhere from Beirut to Byblos.

spicy hummus

Drain and rinse the soaked dried chickpeas and put them in a saucepan. Cover with plenty of water, bring to a boil, and skim until clear. Cover and cook until perfectly soft, about 1 hour.

Strain the chickpeas, reserving ⅓ cup of the cooking liquid. If using canned chickpeas, strain them first and discard the liquid, but use about 4 tablespoons cold water in the food processor.

If the tahini paste appears separated in the jar, mix it properly first. Divide all the ingredients into 2 batches and put the first batch in a food processor, then process briefly. Ideally it should still have some texture and should not be too solid. Taste and adjust the seasoning with salt and pepper and blend again briefly. Transfer to a bowl and repeat with the remaining ingredients.

Drizzle a little oil over the top and sprinkle with fresh cilantro. Serve at room temperature with pita bread or triangles of toasted bread. In the summer, it is better served lightly chilled.

1 cup dried chickpeas, soaked in cold water overnight, or 1 28 oz. can chickpeas

2 tablespoons tahini paste

2 garlic cloves, chopped

freshly squeezed juice of 1–2 lemons

1 tablespoon ground cumin

2 tablespoons extra virgin olive oil

sea salt and freshly ground black pepper

to serve

1 tablespoon extra virgin olive oil

1 tablespoon cilantro, finely chopped

pita bread or triangles of toasted bread

serves 6

4 sprigs of cilantro

4 sprigs of mint

3 oz. gram flour

pinch of turmeric

pinch of sugar

1 egg white

freshly squeezed juice of 1 lime

pinch of salt

8 oz. cauliflower

6 oz. zucchini

1 bunch of baby carrots

vegetable oil, for deep-frying

cilantro chile mint raita

4 sprigs of mint

4 sprigs of cilantro

2 green chiles

½ inch fresh ginger

1 garlic clove, crushed

2 limes

pinch of sea salt

4 tablespoons yogurt

serves 4

Wonderful as party food, these light fritters also make perfect appetizers. Vary the vegetables to suit yourself, and serve with this wonderful raita with a hint of chile.

vegetable fritters
with cilantro chile mint raita

To make the raita, roughly chop the mint and cilantro, and place in a mixing bowl. Seed and chop the chiles. Peel and finely chop the ginger. Add to the bowl with the garlic. Add the grated lime zest and juice, together with the salt and yogurt. Mix and chill until ready to serve.

To make the spicy batter, first chop the cilantro and mint leaves, then put in a bowl with the flour, turmeric, and sugar. Whisk the egg white until stiff, carefully fold in the spiced flour, stir in the lime juice, salt, and enough water to give a light batter.

Break the cauliflower into florets, cut the zucchini into 1 inch slices, and trim the carrots. Heat vegetable oil in a deep-fryer or saucepan.

Dip each piece of vegetable into the batter and deep-fry in hot oil until golden brown. Drain on paper towels. Serve hot with the raita.

Spring rolls are best served immediately after cooking, but to keep last-minute preparation minimal, make the filling up to 24 hours ahead. Fill the spring roll wrappers about an hour before cooking; keep them covered so they remain moist until cooked.

2 tablespoons sunflower oil

2 medium carrots, peeled and cut into matchsticks

½ cup snow peas, cut into matchsticks

¾ cup shiitake mushrooms, chopped

1 inch fresh ginger, peeled and grated

1 small red chile, seeded and chopped

1 cup bean sprouts

2 scallions, thinly sliced

1 tablespoon light soy sauce

2 teaspoons all-purpose flour

8 x 8-inch square spring-roll wrappers

oil for deep-frying

chili dipping sauce

5 tablespoons sweet chili sauce

1 tablespoon light soy sauce

an electric deep-fryer

serves 4 (makes 16)

mini spring rolls
with chili dipping sauce

Heat the sunflower oil in a wok or skillet and stir-fry the carrots, snow peas, mushrooms, and ginger for 1 minute. Add the chopped chile, bean sprouts, and scallions, and stir-fry for 1–2 minutes, or until the vegetables are tender-crisp. Remove from the heat, stir in the soy sauce, and set aside to cool.

Next, make the chili dipping sauce. Mix together the sweet chili sauce and soy sauce in a small bowl and transfer to a serving dish.

In a small bowl, mix the flour with 1 tablespoon water to make a paste. Cut the spring roll wrappers in half diagonally and place under a damp cloth to keep moist. Remove one at a time to fill.

Divide the filling into four and put a quarter of one batch on the long cut side of a wrapper, placing it along the center, slightly in from the edge. Fold over the side flaps. Brush a little flour paste on the pointed end of the wrapper. Roll up towards the point, pressing the end to seal. Repeat with the remaining wrappers. Keep covered until ready to cook.

Fill a deep-fryer with oil to the manufacturer's recommended level. Heat the oil to 350°F and deep-fry the rolls in batches for 2–3 minutes, until crisp and golden. Drain on paper towels. Serve hot with the chili dipping sauce.

Aromatic skewers of meat, fish, vegetables, and poultry are ubiquitous street food all over Southeast Asia—and popular appetizers in restaurants too. Satays are easy to make—great for a party and delicious as part of a grill.

singapore pork satays

Using a sharp knife, cut the pork into ¾-inch slices, then cut each slice into ¾-inch cubes and set aside.

Put the coriander seeds into a dry skillet and heat until aromatic. Grind to a powder with a mortar and pestle. Alternatively, use a spice grinder or clean coffee grinder. Transfer to a wide, shallow bowl, then add the turmeric, salt, and sugar.

Put the lemongrass and shallots into a spice grinder or blender and process until smooth (add a little water, if necessary). Add to the bowl and stir well. Stir in 2 tablespoons of the oil.

Add the cubes of meat and toss to coat with the mixture. Cover and set aside to marinate in the refrigerator for 2 hours or overnight.

Thread 2 pieces of pork onto each soaked wooden skewer and brush with oil. Cook under a preheated hot broiler or over medium hot coals on an outdoor grill until cooked through. Thread a piece of cucumber onto the end of each skewer and serve with the dipping sauce.

2 lb. boneless pork loin

1 tablespoon coriander seeds

½ teaspoon ground turmeric

1 teaspoon salt

1 tablespoon light brown sugar

1 stalk of lemongrass, trimmed and thinly sliced

5 pink Thai shallots or 1 regular, finely chopped

½ cup peanut oil

1 cucumber, quartered lengthwise, seeded, then sliced crosswise

dipping sauce such as soy sauce or nuóc cham (page 22), to serve

20 bamboo skewers, soaked in water for at least 30 minutes

makes 20

1 lb. beef steak

½ cup canned coconut milk

grated zest and freshly squeezed juice of 2 limes

2 red chiles, finely chopped

3 stalks of lemongrass, trimmed and finely chopped

3 garlic cloves, crushed

1 teaspoon ground cumin

2 teaspoons ground coriander

1 teaspoon ground cardamom

2 tablespoons Thai fish sauce, or soy sauce

1 teaspoon sugar

peanut oil, for brushing

dipping sauce, such as soy sauce or nuóc cham (page 22), to serve

10 bamboo skewers, soaked in water for at least 30 minutes

makes about 10

These beef skewers are also delicious made with other meats such as chicken, duck, or pork. You could also serve them with the well-known satay sauce, made with peanuts, which is especially common in Indonesia.

indonesian beef satays

Using a sharp knife, cut the beef crosswise into thin strips, about ⅛ inch thick and 2 inches long. Put the coconut milk, lime zest and juice, chiles, lemongrass, garlic, cumin, coriander, and cardamom into a bowl, then stir in the fish sauce and sugar. Add the beef strips and toss to coat. Cover and chill in the refrigerator for 2 hours or overnight to develop the flavors.

Drain the beef, discarding the marinade. Thread the beef in a zig-zag pattern onto the presoaked skewers and cook under a preheated hot broiler or in a skillet (brushed with a film of peanut oil) until browned and tender. Serve on a platter with a small bowl of dipping sauce.

soups and salads

This is a wonderful meal-in-a-bowl that takes only minutes to put together. It is quite spicy, so reduce the quantity of chile if you prefer. Tom yum paste is a treasure to have in your storecupboard if you have a fondness for Thai food. Use it for stir-fries or Thai curries.

tom yum shrimp noodle soup

4–8 uncooked jumbo shrimp, shells on

2 tablespoons Thai tom yum paste

1 red chile, seeded and finely chopped

1 bell pepper, thinly sliced

3½ oz. brown cap mushrooms, sliced

3½ oz. leeks, trimmed and thinly sliced

3½ oz. rice noodles

freshly squeezed juice of 1 lime

a few cilantro sprigs, to garnish

serves 2–4

Peel the shrimp and use a very sharp knife to cut each one along the back so that it opens out like a butterfly, leaving each shrimp joined along the base and at the tail. Remove the black vein.

Bring 2½ cups water to a boil in a large pan. Stir in the tom yum paste until dissolved. Add the chile, bell pepper, mushrooms, and leeks and let the mixture simmer for 5 minutes.

Meanwhile, put the noodles in a large heatproof bowl, cover with boiling water, and leave to sit for 3–5 minutes until just tender. Drain and spoon into deep serving bowls.

Add the shrimp to the tom yum mixture and simmer for a further 2–3 minutes. Pour the tum yum soup over the noodles. Squeeze a little lime juice over each bowl and garnish with a cilantro sprig. Serve immediately.

4 ears of corn or 2 cups fresh or frozen kernels

2 tablespoons unsalted butter

1 onion, finely chopped

1 small celery stalk, finely chopped

4–5 slices bacon, chopped

5 cups vegetable stock

1 cup light cream

cajun spice blend

¼ teaspoon each of black and white peppercorns

½ teaspoon each of cumin seeds, coriander seeds, cayenne pepper, paprika, and celery salt

to serve

2 tablespoons chopped oregano

an extra pinch of Cajun spice blend

serves 4

Chowders are creamy, chunky soups, the most famous of which is New England clam chowder. Corn chowders are popular too—a real taste of America. This one is inspired by the Deep South: the result is Louisiana soul food with just the right amount of Acadian (Cajun country) spice.

cajun-spiced chowder with corn and bacon

First make the spice blend by crushing the whole spices with a mortar and pestle until coarsely ground. Add the remaining ingredients and mix well.

If using fresh ears of corn, remove the husks and silks and cut the stalk end flat. Put the flat end on a board and cut off the kernels from top to bottom. Discard the cobs.

Melt the butter in a large saucepan, add the onion, and sauté for 5 minutes. Add the celery and sauté for a further 3 minutes until well softened. Add the bacon and cook for 1–2 minutes. Add the corn and Cajun spice blend and mix well.

Add the vegetable stock and bring to a boil. Reduce the heat and simmer for about 35 minutes. Add the cream and simmer until thickened. You can serve the soup immediately or, to thicken it further, put a ladle of the chowder (without any of the bacon) in a blender and purée until smooth. Pour the blended chowder back into the saucepan and mix well.

To serve, ladle into bowls and top with a little oregano and a very light dusting of Cajun spice blend. Serve hot with crusty bread and a green salad.

2 tablespoons extra virgin olive oil

1 medium onion, chopped

3 thin celery stalks, chopped, with leaves reserved

1 large carrot, chopped

2 garlic cloves, chopped

8 oz. chorizo sausage, skinned, halved, then cut into ½ inch slices

14 oz. can chickpeas, drained

7 cups chicken stock

¼ teaspoon hot pimentón (Spanish oak-smoked paprika)

4 oz. spinach, tough stalks removed and leaves coarsely chopped, about 1 cup

¼ teaspoon saffron threads, bruised with a mortar and pestle

serves 4 as an entrée

This hearty soup is a meal in itself. Chunks of chorizo float alongside chickpeas and spinach in a slightly smoky, fragrant broth. The special flavor comes from two typically Spanish spices, pimentón (Spanish oak-smoked paprika, made from a variety of bell pepper) and its homegrown luxury spice, saffron. Although saffron is grown in many parts of the world, it is said that the best comes from La Mancha in Central Spain.

andalusian chickpea soup
with chorizo, paprika, and saffron

Heat the oil in a large saucepan and add the onion, celery, and carrot. Gently sauté the vegetables until they begin to soften. Add the garlic, chorizo, chickpeas, stock, and pimentón. Bring to a boil, reduce the heat, and simmer for about 10 minutes. Add the spinach and celery leaves and simmer for a further 15 minutes.

Add the saffron and clean out the mortar using a little of the stock. (It is a shame to waste even the tiniest speck of expensive saffron!) Add to the saucepan and simmer for another 5 minutes. Serve hot in large, wide bowls as an entrée. This soup is very filling, but some good crusty bread and perhaps some cheese, with the bread or shaved onto the soup, make delightful partners.

singapore turmeric laksa

To make the laksa paste, put all the ingredients in a blender or mortar and pestle and grind to a thick, chunky paste. If using a blender, add a little water to let the blades run.

Heat the oil in a large saucepan and add the laksa paste. Sauté for about 8 minutes. Add the chicken stock, lemongrass, lime leaves and lemon balm, if using, ginger, and soy sauce. Bring to a boil and add the coconut milk, stirring to keep it from separating. Reduce the heat and simmer gently for 15 minutes.

Cook the noodles according to the instructions on the package and drain.

Add the shrimp, bean sprouts, sugar, and salt to the saucepan. Simmer for 2–3 minutes, until the shrimp are just cooked. Discard the lemon balm and lemongrass and add the chopped cilantro.

Seed the cucumber and slice into matchsticks. To serve, put the noodles, cucumber, and Napa cabbage into 4 large or 6 smaller bowls, then ladle over the soup.

Laksa, the spicy shrimp and noodle soup from Malaysia and Singapore, has become fashionable all over the world. This one is a specialty of the Nonya or Straits-Chinese community. Its bright yellow color comes from turmeric and, on its home ground, fresh turmeric is often used rather than the ground turmeric found in the West.

2 tablespoons peanut oil

1½ quarts chicken stock

1 stalk of lemongrass, halved lengthwise

2 kaffir lime leaves (optional)

2 long sprigs of lemon balm (optional)

4 thin slices of fresh ginger or galangal

1 teaspoon light soy sauce

1¾ cups canned coconut milk

8 oz. thick Chinese egg noodles

1 lb. uncooked shrimp, shelled and deveined

4 oz. (about 1 cup) bean sprouts, rinsed and trimmed

brown sugar or palm sugar, to taste

sea salt

a bunch of cilantro, chopped

laksa paste

6 shallots, coarsely chopped

4 red chiles, seeded and chopped

1 stalk lemongrass, trimmed and chopped

1 teaspoon ground turmeric

1 garlic clove, chopped

½ teaspoon ground ginger or galangal

½ teaspoon anchovy paste

6 macadamia nuts or 12 almonds

1 kaffir lime leaf (optional)

2 tablespoons Thai fish sauce

to serve

4 inches cucumber

a handful of shredded Napa cabbage

serves 4–6

1½ lb. trimmed stewing beef, cut into small chunks

7 white peppercorns

1 inch fresh galangal, peeled and sliced, or fresh ginger

1 teaspoon freshly grated nutmeg

¼ teaspoon ground turmeric

14 oz. canned coconut milk

sea salt

spice paste

2–3 tablespoons peanut oil

1 teaspoon ground coriander

7 white peppercorns

4 red bird's eye chiles

2 teaspoons brown or palm sugar

1 garlic clove, chopped

5 fresh Thai basil (or sweet basil) leaves

a large handful of cilantro, about 1 oz., coarsely chopped

8 pink Thai shallots or 1 regular shallot

a few cardamom seeds (not pods)

1 inch fresh ginger, peeled and chopped

1 teaspoon anchovy paste

1 tablespoon fish sauce

serves 4–6

This strongly spiced and flavored soup has slices of meat swimming in plenty of creamy broth. It is quintessentially Indonesian in its spicing; living on the world's largest archipelago and comprising around 350 ethnic groups, Indonesians are a varied people and so is their cuisine.

indonesian beef and coconut soup

Put all the spice paste ingredients into a blender or a food processor and grind to a thick paste, adding a dash of water to let the blades run. Set aside.

Put the beef, peppercorns, galangal, nutmeg, turmeric, and salt into a saucepan, add 1½ quarts water and bring to a boil, skimming off the foam as it rises to the surface. Stir, reduce the heat, and simmer uncovered for about 1½ hours, until the meat is mostly tender and the stock is well reduced.

Strain the beef, discarding the galangal slices and peppercorns, but reserving the stock. Return the stock to the pan, then stir in the spice paste. Bring to a boil, reduce the heat, add the beef, and simmer for 5 minutes, stirring regularly.

Finally, add the coconut milk and simmer gently for a few minutes. Serve the soup on its own or with a small mound of plain rice.

2 garlic cloves

1 teaspoon coarse kosher salt or sea salt

1 large cucumber, peeled and coarsely chopped

1 yellow bell pepper, seeded and coarsely chopped

2 celery stalks, coarsely chopped

4 ripe tomatoes, coarsely chopped

1 red onion, coarsely chopped

4 cups fresh tomato juice

2 teaspoons cumin seeds, pan-toasted

1 teaspoon mild chili powder

1 ripe avocado, halved and pitted

freshly squeezed juice of 2 limes

freshly ground black pepper

cilantro leaves set in ice cubes, or chopped cilantro, to serve

serves 6

Ice-cold and enhanced with avocado, lime, cumin, and chili, this gazpacho is refreshingly hard to beat on a hot summer's day. If you have time, freeze cilantro leaves in ice cubes and use them to decorate your soup.

mexican gazpacho

Using a mortar and pestle, pound the garlic with the salt until puréed. Put the cucumber, bell pepper, celery, tomatoes, and onion in a bowl, add the puréed garlic, and mix well. Transfer half of the mixture to a food processor and pulse until chopped but still slightly chunky. Pour into a large bowl. Purée the remaining mixture until smooth, then add to the bowl. Mix in the tomato juice, cumin, chili powder, and freshly ground black pepper to taste.

Chill for several hours until very cold or overnight. If short of time, put the soup in the freezer for 30 minutes to chill.

Cut the avocado into small cubes, toss in the lime juice until well coated, then stir into the gazpacho.

To serve, ladle the soup into chilled bowls, then add a few ice cubes or sprinkle with chopped cilantro.

This makes a lovely change from shrimp cocktail! Buy the juiciest-looking cooked shrimp you can find and leave them in the marinade for as long as possible. If it is available, use pink grapefruit; it looks prettier and tastes sweeter than the white variety.

spicy tiger shrimp salad

1 garlic clove, crushed

freshly squeezed juice of 1 lime

2 tablespoons sweet chili sauce

7 oz. cooked tiger shrimp, peeled but tails left intact

1 pink grapefruit

2 tablespoons extra virgin olive oil

¾ cup cherry tomatoes, halved

1 small ripe avocado, peeled, pitted, and diced

½ red onion, thinly sliced

a handful of cilantro leaves

serves 2

Put the garlic, lime juice, and sweet chili sauce in a shallow container and whisk with a fork to combine. Add the shrimp, stir to coat with the mixture, cover, and set aside to marinate while you prepare the rest of the salad.

Cut away the peel and pith from the grapefruit with a serrated knife. Hold the grapefruit in the palm of your hand and cut away each segment, working over a large bowl to catch the juices.

Add the olive oil to the grapefruit juice and whisk with a fork to combine. Add the grapefruit segments, cherry tomatoes, avocado, red onion, and cilantro to the bowl and toss to combine.

Divide the prepared salad between 2 serving plates. Remove the shrimp from their marinade (using tongs or a slotted spoon) and arrange them on top. Drizzle the remaining marinade over the salad. Serve immediately with slices of warm garlic bread or similar.

14 oz. canned chickpeas, drained and rinsed

3½ oz. canned red kidney beans, drained and rinsed

1 red onion, finely chopped

2 red chiles, seeded and finely chopped

2 tablespoons basil leaves, torn

1½ tablespoons chopped flat leaf parsley

a small bunch of chives, finely chopped

8 oz. grilled chicken breast, chopped

8 oz. very ripe cherry tomatoes, halved

2 inches cucumber, chopped

fresh Parmesan cheese shavings

dressing

2 tablespoons extra virgin olive oil

¼ cup balsamic vinegar

2–3 garlic cloves, crushed

1 teaspoon whole-grain mustard

sea salt and freshly ground black pepper

serves 4

The great thing about this salad is you can eat it any time of the day, hot or cold. Because the beans hold their shape, it travels well, too. So if you make a bit too much for dinner, just put it in an airtight container and take it with you the next day for lunch.

chicken and chile
chickpea salad

To make the dressing, put the oil, vinegar, garlic, and mustard in a salad bowl. Season with salt and pepper, to taste, and stir to mix. Add the chickpeas, kidney beans, onion, chiles, and herbs and mix well. Cover and chill in the refrigerator for 2–4 hours to let the flavors infuse.

When ready to eat, add the chicken, tomatoes, and cucumber to the salad. Season with salt and pepper, to taste, and toss well. Sprinkle with a few shavings of Parmesan. This is good served with warm pita bread.

20 uncooked tiger shrimp

1 tablespoon sesame seeds

1 tablespoon chopped cilantro

marinade

1 inch fresh ginger, peeled and grated

1–2 red chiles, seeded and chopped

¼ cup freshly squeezed lime juice

1 tablespoon olive oil

2 tablespoons light soy sauce

½ teaspoon brown sugar

1–2 garlic cloves, crushed

mango salad

3 oz. bok choy, shredded

1 large ripe mango, peeled, pitted, and chopped

2½ oz. bean sprouts

½ medium cucumber, chopped

1 red bell pepper, seeded and thinly sliced

1 bunch scallions, trimmed and chopped

freshly ground black pepper

serves 4

This salad is a really tasty, light dinner and makes a great barbecue dish, too. You can replace the tiger shrimp with monkfish, skinned, boned, and cut into small pieces, if you want to ring the changes.

shrimp and mango salad

Peel the shrimp and, if necessary, discard the thin black vein that runs down the back. Rinse and pat dry with paper towels. Put in a shallow dish.

To make the marinade, put the ginger, chiles, lime juice, oil, soy sauce, sugar, and garlic in a bowl. Mix well. Pour the marinade over the shrimp, stir, then cover. Refrigerate and let marinate for 15–30 minutes.

Meanwhile, prepare the salad. Put the bok choy and mango in a serving bowl. Add the bean sprouts, cucumber, red bell pepper, scallions, and black pepper, to taste. Mix well and reserve.

Drain the shrimp, reserving the marinade. Heat a nonstick sauté pan or wok, add the shrimp, and cook, stirring frequently, for 2–3 minutes, or until pink. Add to the mango salad.

Pour the marinade into a small saucepan. Bring to a boil and boil for 2 minutes. Pour the marinade over the salad and toss lightly. Sprinkle with the sesame seeds and cilantro and serve immediately.

This salad is very simple and you can also make it with cooked shrimp. When preparing the lemongrass and kaffir lime leaves, make sure to chop them very finely indeed. If you can't find them, use a squeeze of lemon juice and some grated lime zest instead.

thai spicy shrimp salad

Heat the oil in a wok or large, heavy skillet, add the shrimp, and stir-fry for about 1 minute until opaque. Let cool.

Put the dressing ingredients in a bowl and beat well with a fork until the sugar dissolves. Add the shrimp and all the other ingredients except the mint sprigs. Toss, then serve, topped with mint.

1 tablespoon peanut oil

12 uncooked medium shrimp, shelled, deveined, and halved lengthwise

1 stalk lemongrass, very finely chopped

a handful of cilantro leaves, finely chopped

2 pink Thai shallots or 1 small regular shallot, finely sliced lengthwise

3 scallions, finely chopped

1 red chile, finely sliced and seeded if preferred

2 kaffir lime leaves, very finely chopped

12 cherry tomatoes, halved

a handful of mint sprigs, to serve

thai dressing

4 tablespoons Thai fish sauce

freshly squeezed juice of 1 lemon or 2 limes

2 teaspoons brown sugar

2 tablespoons Thai red curry paste

serves 4

Poaching is a very healthy way of cooking the chicken in this salad: there is no added fat, and much of what's there melts away as the chicken cooks. This salad isn't authentic —that would involve stir-fried chicken mince—but it's easy and it tastes fresh and good, like most Vietnamese food. If you can't find Vietnamese mint, substitute ordinary mint, but you can't use ordinary basil instead of Asian basil— just leave it out.

vietnamese chicken salad with chili-lime dressing

Put the chicken in a wide saucepan, add the ginger, garlic, fish sauce, chile, and scallions. Add chicken stock or water to cover and return to a boil. Reduce the heat, cover with a lid, and simmer, without boiling, until the chicken is tender, about 15–20 minutes. Remove from the heat and let cool in the liquid. Remove from the liquid, take the meat off the bone, discard bone and skin, then pull the chicken into long shreds. Reserve the cooking liquid for another use, such as soup.

Put all the dressing ingredients in a screw-top bottle and shake to mix.

To prepare the carrot, peel and shred into long matchsticks on a mandoline or the large blade of a box grater.

Pile the bean sprouts on 4 plates. Add the carrot and chicken and top with the scallions, mint, and basil leaves, if using. Sprinkle with the dressing and roasted peanuts, then serve.

2 chicken breasts, on the bone

1 inch fresh ginger, sliced

1 garlic clove, crushed

1 tablespoon fish sauce or a pinch of salt

1 red chile, sliced

2 scallions, sliced

boiling chicken stock or water, to cover

1 small carrot

4 handfuls of bean sprouts, rinsed and drained

6 scallions, halved, then finely sliced lengthwise

a handful of fresh mint leaves, preferably Vietnamese mint

a handful of Asian basil leaves (optional)

2 tablespoons roasted peanuts, finely chopped

chili-lime dressing

1/3 cup freshly squeezed lime juice, about 2–3 limes

1 tablespoon fish sauce

2 tablespoons brown sugar

1 green chile, halved, seeded, and finely chopped

1 red chile, halved, seeded, and finely chopped

1 garlic clove, crushed

1 inch fresh ginger, peeled and grated

serves 4

8 leaves of Napa cabbage

1 large carrot

1 cucumber, about 8 inches long, halved, seeded, cut into 2 inch sections, then finely sliced lengthwise

6 scallions, sliced diagonally

8 slices dried mango, chopped

1/2 cup cashews, toasted in a dry skillet, then coarsely crushed

tamarind dressing

2 teaspoons tamarind concentrate

1/2 teaspoon Szechuan peppercorns, lightly toasted in a dry skillet, then coarsely crushed

2 teaspoons toasted sesame oil

1 garlic clove, finely chopped

1/2 teaspoon brown or palm sugar, to taste

about 2 tablespoons chopped Thai basil, Vietnamese mint, or cilantro

sea salt

serves 4

A simple vegetarian salad with fragrant Southeast Asian flavors. It is versatile too, because other ingredients can be added according to the season. Sour tamarind and Szechuan pepper form an unusual partnership in the dressing—a combination of sour and hot.

vegetarian cashew salad
with tamarind dressing

First make the dressing. Mix the tamarind concentrate with 1 cup warm water. Put it, the Szechuan pepper, sesame oil, garlic, sugar, and chopped herbs into a screw-top bottle and shake well. Set aside.

Stack the Napa cabbage leaves on top of each other and slice them finely. Grate the carrot into long sticks using the large blade of a box grater, or slice thinly into long strips. Divide the shredded leaves between 4 plates, add a layer of grated carrot, then the cucumber strips. Top with the scallions and dried mango. Sprinkle the dressing over the salad, top with the cashews, then serve.

Variations Instead of Napa cabbage leaves, use other crisp leaves such as romaine. For a non-vegetarian version, add 2 poached boneless and skinless chicken breasts, cooled and pulled into shreds, or 2 duck breasts, cooked in a stove-top grill pan, then sliced.

4 oz. green beans, trimmed

2 cups finely shredded red or white cabbage

3 plum tomatoes, halved lengthwise, seeded, and sliced

4 scallions, sliced

4 cup-shaped lettuce leaves, to serve (optional)

⅓ cup roasted peanuts, coarsely ground

dressing

a handful of cilantro

2 red serrano chiles, seeded

2 garlic cloves, chopped

2 tablespoons light soy sauce

2 tablespoons freshly squeezed lime juice

2 tablespoons palm sugar or soft brown sugar

serves 4

This hybrid Thai coleslaw is based on the classic som tum, usually made from grated green papaya (when unripe, the fruit is firm, crunchy, and perfect for grating). Green papaya is not the easiest ingredient to find, so red cabbage is used instead. The word "coleslaw" comes from koolsla— Dutch for "cabbage salad." Here, these two classic dishes become a salad with a delicious new twist.

thai coleslaw

To make the dressing, reserve a few cilantro leaves, then put the rest in a blender or food processor. Add the chiles, garlic, soy sauce, lime juice, and sugar and blend until smooth. Set aside.

Blanch the beans in boiling water for 2 minutes, then refresh in cold water. Mix the cabbage, beans, tomatoes, and scallions in a bowl. Pour the dressing on top, toss well to coat, and let marinate for about 30 minutes.

Spoon into bowls lined with the lettuce leaves, if using, sprinkle with the ground peanuts and the reserved cilantro leaves, then serve.

You can alter the vegetables in this salad according to what's in season. Try broccoli or carrots sliced lengthwise into matchsticks, spinach leaves, sliced Napa cabbage, or cauliflower florets. Green beans keep their crunch well, so are good for this salad.

indonesian gado-gado

To make the peanut sauce, toast the peanuts in a dry skillet. Transfer to a dish towel, rub off the skins, then put the nuts in a blender. Grind to a coarse meal, then add the chiles, onion, garlic, salt, sugar, and coconut milk. Blend to a purée, then transfer to a saucepan and cook, stirring, until thickened.

Thinly slice the halved cucumbers diagonally, put on a plate, sprinkle with salt, set aside for 10 minutes, then rinse and pat dry with paper towels. Chill.

Cook the beans in boiling salted water until al dente, then drain, rinse immediately under cold running water, then transfer to a bowl of ice water. Just before serving, drain again and pat dry with paper towels.

Peel the pepper with a vegetable peeler, cut off and discard the top and bottom, then halve, seed, and finely slice lengthwise.

Heat 2 tablespoons peanut oil in a skillet, add the tofu, and cook until brown on both sides, then drain and slice thickly.

To cook the shrimp crackers, fill a wok or heavy kettle one-third full with peanut oil and heat to 375°F. Drop in 1 cracker to test the temperature—it should puff up immediately. Add the crackers, crowding them so they curl up, then cook until puffed and golden, about 3 seconds. Remove and drain on paper towels.

To cook the onion rings, reheat the oil, add the sliced onion, and deep-fry until crisp and golden. Remove and drain on paper towels.

Arrange the cucumbers, beans, pepper, tofu, bean sprouts, lettuce leaves, daikon, and quartered eggs on a large platter. Top with the onion rings and shrimp crackers, drizzle with the peanut sauce, sprinkle with salt, and serve.

2 small cucumbers, such as Kirby, halved lengthwise and seeded

8 Chinese long beans or green beans, cut into 2 inch lengths

1 orange or red bell pepper

peanut oil, for cooking

2 firm tofu cakes

20–25 shrimp crackers

2 red onions, thinly sliced into rings

a large handful of bean sprouts, rinsed, drained, and trimmed

8 small leaves romaine lettuce

6 inches daikon, peeled and sliced into matchstick lengths

2 hard-cooked eggs, quartered

kosher salt or sea salt flakes

peanut sauce

1½ cups shelled fresh peanuts

2 red chiles, halved, seeded, and finely chopped

2 bird's eye chiles, halved, seeded, and finely chopped

1 onion, finely chopped

1 garlic clove, crushed

1 teaspoon kosher salt or sea salt

2 teaspoons brown sugar

²⁄₃ cup coconut milk

serves 4

1 quart coconut milk (about 4 cans)

8 oz. somen or cellophane noodles

4 tablespoons peanut oil

1 lb. boneless chicken, cut in
½-inch strips

1 small package bean sprouts, trimmed

4 scallions, sliced diagonally

1 red chile, seeded and finely sliced

sea salt

sprigs of mint and cilantro, to serve

spice paste

4 red or orange chiles (not habaneros)

3 stalks lemongrass, finely sliced

1 inch fresh galangal or ginger, sliced

1 teaspoon ground turmeric

4 candlenuts or 8 almonds, crushed

1 teaspoon shrimp paste*

1 garlic clove, chopped

4 shallots or 2 mild onions, sliced

1 tablespoon coriander seeds

serves 4

Laksas are one-bowl meals from Malaysia and Singapore. The spice paste usually contains candlenuts, but if you can't find any, use almonds or macadamias instead.

singapore coconut laksa

Open the cans of coconut milk and pour the thick and thin bits into separate bowls. Put all the spice paste ingredients into a spice grinder or clean coffee grinder and work to a mush, in batches if necessary.

If using somen noodles, cook in boiling salted water for 2½–3 minutes. Add a splash of cold water from time to time, then return to a boil. If using cellophane noodles, soak in hot water for 15 minutes, then boil for 1 minute before serving.

Heat the oil in a wok, add the chicken, and stir-fry until lightly golden and cooked through. Remove from the wok and set aside. Add the spice paste and cook, stirring until aromatic—about 6–8 minutes.

Add the thin coconut milk, bring to a boil, stirring, add the cooked chicken, and return to a boil, still stirring. Add the thick part of the coconut milk, bean sprouts, scallions, chile, and salt to taste, and cook gently, stirring, until well heated (keep stirring or the coconut milk will curdle).

Serve in large soup bowls with sprigs of mint and cilantro.

*Note Shrimp paste is sold in Asian stores, and must be either covered and heated in a microwave first, or wrapped in foil and broiled for a few minutes. If unavailable, use a similar quantity of Thai fish sauce, or anchovy essence.

The spice paste in this recipe can be made in quantity and frozen—a useful standby. You can use a ready-made Thai curry paste to save time, if you like. The tamarind gives this laksa a lemony taste.

tamarind fish laksa

If using dried noodles, cook in boiling salted water for 10–12 minutes; if fresh, boil for 2–2½ minutes. During boiling, add a splash of cold water once or twice during the cooking time, then return to a boil. Drain and cover with cold water until ready to assemble the dish.

Put all the spice paste ingredients, except the peanut oil, in a blender, spice grinder, or small food processor and work to a purée, adding a few tablespoons of water as necessary to make a paste. Heat the oil in a wok, add the paste, and stir-fry for about 6 minutes until the rawness is cooked out of the spices.

Add the stock and ginger and heat until boiling, add the fish, turn off the heat, and put on the lid. Leave for about 5 minutes until the fish is cooked, then break the fish into large pieces in the stock. Reheat to boiling point, then stir in the tamarind concentrate, sugar, and salt and pepper to taste.

Drain the noodles, then dunk them and the shrimp, if using, into boiling water until heated through. Drain, then put a pile of the hot noodles and shrimp in 4 large Chinese soup bowls, ladle the fish and stock over the top, and sprinkle with mint, bean sprouts, cilantro, and chiles.

1 lb. fresh udon noodles, or 8 oz. dried

1 quart fish stock or water

1 inch fresh ginger or galangal, grated

1 lb. skinless, boneless fish fillets

1 tablespoon tamarind concentrate or freshly squeezed juice of 1 lime

1 teaspoon brown sugar or palm sugar

sea salt and freshly ground black pepper

spice paste

3 dried chiles, deseeded and soaked

2 stalks lemongrass, chopped

1 inch fresh ginger or galangal, peeled and grated

1 teaspoon ground turmeric

1 tablespoon shrimp paste (see note page 77)

12 scallions, thinly sliced

1 tablespoon peanut oil

to serve

8–12 cooked, peeled shrimp (optional)

1 bunch Vietnamese mint or mint

1 small package bean sprouts, trimmed

1 bunch cilantro leaves, torn

2 red chiles, seeded and thinly sliced

serves 4

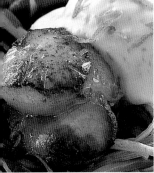

fish and seafood

This fast, flavorsome supper is ideal as a light main course. If you want to reduce preparation time further, you can use two 12 oz. packages of any prepared stir-fry vegetables—such as red bell peppers, bean sprouts, and zucchini—instead of the leeks, carrots, and onion.

chili scallops with leeks
and lime crème fraîche

First make the lime crème fraîche. Put the crème fraîche in a small bowl, add the chopped cilantro and grated lime zest and juice, and season with salt and pepper. Set aside.

Heat 1 tablespoon of the oil in a large nonstick skillet or wok and stir-fry the bacon lardons until golden. Remove from the pan with a slotted spoon, drain, and set aside on paper towels. In the remaining fat stir-fry the leeks, carrots, onion, chiles, and garlic until soft and golden brown. Add the honey and soy sauce, transfer to a bowl or plate, and keep warm.

Rinse the pan under running water and wipe dry. Add the remaining oil and heat until scorching hot. Season the scallops with pepper and fry briefly on both sides in the pan, allowing around 1½ minutes on each side; they should be firm-textured after cooking. Remove from the pan once cooked and keep warm.

Return the vegetable mixture and bacon lardons to the pan and reheat until piping hot. Divide the vegetables between 4 serving plates, top with 4 scallops per plate, and add a generous spoonful of the lime crème fraîche. Garnish each with a cilantro sprig and serve immediately.

2 tablespoons safflower oil

3 slices thick-sliced bacon, cut into lardons (thin strips)

2 large leeks, trimmed and cut into strips

2 oz. carrots, peeled and cut into strips

1 large onion, thinly sliced

2 red chiles, seeded and finely chopped

2 garlic cloves, crushed

2 tablespoons honey

2 tablespoons soy sauce

16 large scallops

sea salt and freshly ground black pepper

lime crème fraîche

⅔ cup crème fraîche

2 tablespoons chopped cilantro, plus extra sprigs to garnish

finely grated zest of 1 lime

1 tablespoon freshly squeezed lime juice

serves 4

1 tablespoon olive oil

1 cup basmati rice

1 large onion, chopped

1 teaspoon ground turmeric

14 oz. canned chopped tomatoes

1 large red bell pepper, seeded
and finely chopped

1–2 garlic cloves, chopped

2 cups chicken stock

14 oz. canned butter beans, drained
and rinsed

1–2 red chiles, seeded and thinly sliced

1 lb. cooked peeled shrimp, thawed
if frozen

3 tablespoons cilantro, coarsely chopped

sea salt and freshly ground black pepper

serves 4

This makes a great midweek supper dish, and it is an easy way to increase your vegetable intake by adding vegetables of your choice. Try throwing in some freezer staples such as frozen peas, corn, or green beans. They cook in minutes and don't require any preparation.

shrimp and butter bean rice

Heat the oil in a large nonstick saucepan. Add the rice, onion, and turmeric and cook over medium heat, stirring, for 2 minutes. Add the tomatoes, pepper, garlic, stock, and salt and pepper, to taste. Cover the pan with a tight-fitting lid, reduce the heat, and simmer for 15 minutes, until most of the stock has been absorbed by the rice.

Add the butter beans, chiles, and shrimp to the rice mixture and stir through gently. Replace the lid and cook for a further 3 minutes, or until the stock is absorbed and the shrimp are thoroughly warmed through. Stir in the cilantro and serve immediately.

Variation Brown four skinned, boneless chicken thighs then add to the rice and onion and proceed as above. Add some frozen peas and corn kernels with the butter beans and shrimp and cook for 3–5 minutes, or until cooked and piping hot. Serve with lemon wedges, if you like.

Salmon cutlets and plenty of fresh vegetables make this a delicious, healthy meal. As a variation, exchange the leeks for thinly sliced zucchini and add some snow peas and tiny broccoli florets. If you like, try using oyster or fresh shiitake mushrooms and add some shredded Napa cabbage leaves or bok choy.

asian salmon
with rice noodles

Wash the salmon steaks and pat dry with paper towels. Rub the five-spice powder into both sides of the fish and season well with black pepper. Set aside for 30 minutes.

Meanwhile, put the noodles in a bowl, cover with boiling water, and let soak for 15 minutes. Drain, then add the noodles to a saucepan of boiling water, and cook for 1 minute. Drain and keep the noodles warm.

Cook the salmon cutlets under a hot broiler for 7–10 minutes, or until thoroughly cooked, turning once halfway through the cooking time.

Heat a nonstick sauté pan. Add the soy sauce, honey, ginger, garlic, carrot, and leek to the pan and sauté the vegetables for 3–4 minutes, until beginning to soften. Add the mushrooms to the pan and sauté for a further 2 minutes.

Divide the noodles between 4 bowls or plates. Spoon the vegetables and their juices over the noodles and put the grilled salmon on top. Sprinkle with cilantro, if using, and serve.

4 salmon steaks, about 4 oz. each

2 teaspoons Chinese five-spice powder

10 oz. rice vermicelli noodles

2 tablespoons light soy sauce

2 teaspoons honey

1 inch fresh ginger, peeled and grated

2 garlic cloves, crushed

1 large carrot, thinly sliced

1 large leek, sliced

12 oz. mushrooms, wiped and sliced

1 tablespoon chopped cilantro (optional)

freshly ground black pepper

serves 4

If you have friends coming round for a midweek supper and you need to make something special but don't want to spend more than 10 minutes in the kitchen, this recipe is the answer. Any other seafood, such as baby squid, would also work well in this recipe.

chili scallops with spaghetti

Rinse the scallops in cold water and pat dry on paper towels. If the scallops are large, cut them into 2 or 3 slices.

Bring a large saucepan of water to a boil. Add a pinch of salt, then the spaghetti, and cook until al dente or according to the timings on the package. Drain the spaghetti, reserving 2 tablespoons of the cooking water. Return the pasta and the reserved cooking water to the warm pan.

Put the garlic, chiles, and cilantro in a small bowl and mix. Heat a heavy-based sauté pan and add 1 tablespoon of the oil. Add the chile mixture to the pan and cook for 1 minute, stirring, then add the scallops. Stir well until coated with the oil and chiles. Cook, stirring occasionally, for 2–3 minutes, until the scallops are cooked. Season to taste and keep warm in a low oven.

Add the cream and remaining oil to the spaghetti and heat gently, stirring frequently, until piping hot. Serve immediately, topped with the scallops.

16–24 sea scallops

1 lb. spaghetti

4 garlic cloves, coarsely chopped

1–2 red chiles, seeded and coarsely chopped

1 tablespoon chopped cilantro

2 tablespoons extra virgin olive oil

½ cup light cream

sea salt and freshly ground black pepper

serves 4

4 tuna steaks, 6 oz. each

2–3 garlic cloves, crushed

1 teaspoon ground cumin

2 teaspoons finely grated lime zest

1 tablespoon freshly squeezed lime juice

2 teaspoons olive oil

1 teaspoon ground coriander

freshly ground black pepper

pepper noodles

7 oz. egg noodles

1 teaspoon sunflower oil

1 garlic clove, chopped

1 red bell pepper, seeded and
thinly sliced

1 yellow bell pepper, seeded and
thinly sliced

finely grated zest and juice of 1 lime

1 tablespoon light soy sauce

sea salt and freshly ground black pepper

to serve

1 red bell pepper, chopped

2 tablespoons chopped cilantro

4 lime wedges

serves 4

Fresh tuna, unlike canned tuna, is a good source of those all-important omega-3 fatty acids, which help to protect against heart disease. Don't overcook the tuna because it can become quite dry and chewy. Fresh tuna is at its most tender when it is still pink in the middle.

spicy tuna steaks
with pepper noodles

Wipe the tuna or lightly rinse and pat dry with paper towels. Put the garlic, cumin, lime zest, lime juice, oil, ground coriander, and black pepper in a small bowl. Mix to make a paste. Spread the paste thinly on both sides of the tuna steaks and leave to marinate for at least 15 minutes.

Heat a nonstick sauté pan until hot and press the tuna steaks into the pan to seal them. Lower the heat and cook for 3 minutes. Turn the fish over and cook for a further 3–5 minutes, until cooked to personal preference. Remove from the pan, transfer to a plate, and keep warm in a low oven.

To make the pepper noodles, bring a large saucepan of water to a boil. Add the noodles and cook for 4 minutes, or according to the timings on the package. Drain, rinse, and reserve. Heat a nonstick sauté pan, add the oil, garlic, and peppers and sauté gently, until the vegetables start to soften. Add the drained noodles, the lime zest and juice, and soy sauce. Cook for 1–2 minutes, turning frequently, until warmed through.

Transfer the noodles to warm serving plates and top with the tuna steaks. Sprinkle with some chopped red pepper and cilantro. Add a wedge of lime and serve immediately.

Variation Try a different marinade for the tuna: blend 2 crushed garlic cloves with 1 seeded and finely chopped chile, 2 teaspoons of freshly grated fresh ginger, 2 tablespoons of chopped cilantro, 1 teaspoon of Thai fish sauce, and 1 tablespoon of olive oil. Marinate as above.

Use the large, dried red New Mexico chiles if you can get them. They are available in specialist shops and by mail order. Alternatively, substitute one small dried red chile (much hotter than the New Mexico version). Mussels are naturally salty, so take care when seasoning this recipe. This is good served with toasted sourdough bread.

steamed mussels
in a red chili broth

Roast the garlic and tomatoes in a preheated oven at 300°F for 1 hour.

To make the broth, soak the chiles in the stock and ⅔ cup water for about 1 hour until softened and limp. Puree in a blender and set aside.

Heat 1 tablespoon of the olive oil in a pan and sauté the garlic and tomato until reheated. Add the mussels, stir in the broth, cover, and steam for about 5 to 7 minutes until the mussels have opened. Discard any that remain closed. Taste and adjust the seasoning. Stir in the cream, if using, and serve immediately with a sprinkling of ground paprika.

2 garlic cloves

4 red tomatoes, sliced

2 dried red New Mexico chiles, seeded

1¼ cups fish stock

2 tablespoons olive oil

2 lb. mussels, scrubbed and debearded

⅔ cup light cream (optional)

salt and freshly ground black pepper

ground paprika, to serve

serves 4

1 cup canned coconut milk

1 Thai red chile, seeded and sliced

1 Thai green chile, seeded and sliced

2 stalks of lemongrass, cut in half lengthwise

1 lb. mussels, scrubbed and debearded

1 lb. monkfish, cod, or similar firm-fleshed fish

1 lb. uncooked tiger shrimp, shelled and deveined

leaves from 1 bunch of cilantro, torn

serves 4

Thai fish curries taste clean and fresh, and are absolutely packed with spicy flavor. It's important not to overcook the seafood, so remove it from the broth as soon as it is cooked, then reheat just before serving.

thai seafood curry
with cilantro and coconut milk

Pour the coconut milk into a pan, add the chiles and lemongrass, and bring to a boil. Add the mussels and remove as soon as they open. Add the fish and the tiger shrimp and poach gently until the shrimp change color and the fish becomes opaque.

Remove the fish and shrimp from the pan and set aside with the mussels. Gently pull the fish into bite-size pieces.

Return the coconut milk to a boil and reduce by half. Return the seafood to the pan and reheat, then serve sprinkled with torn cilantro leaves and accompanied by fragrant Thai rice or pasta.

You can adapt this recipe for the grill—the woodsmoke adds a wonderful depth of flavor. Always cook the shrimp with their shells on, again for extra flavor.

shrimp brochettes with chile, papaya, and mango salsa

To make the salsa, mix the ingredients together in a small container, cover, and chill for up to 6 hours.

Place the shrimp in a bowl and sprinkle over the chili oil and lime juice. Marinate for 1 to 2 hours.

Thread a wedge of red onion onto each skewer, then thread on the shrimp, followed by a slice of lime. Brush with the marinade, sprinkle with sea salt, then cook under a preheated broiler or on a grill for a few minutes on each side.

Garnish with wedges of lime and onion, the sliced chile, and torn cilantro leaves, together with the salsa spooned over or served separately. Rice, pita bread, or salad would be suitable accompaniments.

24 uncooked, unpeeled shrimp

1 teaspoon chili oil

freshly squeezed juice of 2 limes, plus 1 lime, sliced, and 1 lime, quartered

1 large red onion, cut into 8 wedges

sea salt

chile, papaya, and mango salsa

1 large ripe mango, peeled, pitted, and diced

1 ripe papaya, about 8 oz., peeled, seeded, and diced

1 tablespoon balsamic vinegar

1 tablespoon chopped red chiles

salt and freshly ground black pepper

to serve

1 red chile, sliced

cilantro leaves

4 wooden skewers, soaked in water for at least 30 minutes

serves 4

The piri piri is a fiercely hot chile introduced to Africa by the Portuguese. The name is also used for the hot sauces in which the pods are used. Versions of piri piri sauce can be found from Mozambique and Angola to Brazil, as well as in Portugal itself. For this recipe, use any hot, thin, red chiles. Nigella seeds are not a traditional component of piri piri recipes, but they add a special flavor and texture.

african seafood kabobs
with piri piri basting oil

To make the piri piri basting oil, put the garlic, chiles, lemon juice and olive oil into a blender and blend until smooth. Transfer to a bowl and stir in the nigella seeds, if using.

Dip the shrimp and scallops into the basting oil and coat well. Thread the shrimp and scallops alternately onto the skewers, with the bay leaves between them.

Set apart on a broiler rack over a broiler tray. Cook at high heat under a preheated broiler for about 5 minutes or until done, turning once during cooking. (Don't overcook or the scallops will be tough—shrimp and scallops are done when the flesh becomes opaque.) Brush with the piri piri basting oil several times while the skewers are cooking. Alternatively, put the remaining oil into a small saucepan, boil for 1–2 minutes, then serve as a dipping sauce. Serve the kabobs with ciabatta or focaccia bread.

12 large, uncooked shrimp, peeled, but with tail fins intact

8–12 small sea scallops, muscles removed

12–20 bay leaves

piri piri basting oil

3 garlic cloves, crushed

5–6 red bird's eye chiles or 8–9 regular red chiles, seeded and coarsely chopped

freshly squeezed juice of ½ lemon

⅓–½ cup extra virgin olive oil

½ teaspoon nigella seeds (optional)

4 metal skewers

serves 4

Chermoula is a spicy Moroccan sauce or marinade for fish. In Tangier, huge baskets of spices and herbs, such as the cilantro and cumin for chermoula, are lined up for sale in the souks. The color of this sauce is produced by fresh cilantro, while the chili powder gives it a kick. It can be used as both a marinade and a topping.

moroccan grilled fish
with chermoula spice paste

To make the chermoula, put the cilantro and garlic into a blender or food processor. Add the pimentón, cumin, chili powder, olive oil, lemon juice, and a pinch of salt and blend to a smooth paste—if necessary, add a dash of water to let the blades run. Alternatively, use a mortar and pestle.

About 30 minutes before cooking the fish, sprinkle it with salt, put a spoonful of chermoula onto each steak and rub all over. Set aside to marinate.

When ready to cook, brush a stove-top grill pan with olive oil and heat over medium-high heat until very hot. Add the fish to the pan and cook for 1–2 minutes, depending on thickness. Don't move the fish until it loosens and will move without sticking. Turn it over and continue cooking for 1–2 minutes more. If the fish is very thick, cook for 1 minute longer, but do not overcook or the flesh will be tough. (If you have a small pan, cook in batches of 1 or 2 and keep them warm in a very low oven while you cook the remainder.)

To serve, top each fish steak with the remaining chermoula and extra cilantro.

If you would like to serve the fish with typical North African accompaniments, roast some butternut squash or sweet potatoes with olive oil and cinnamon, and make some fluffy couscous, with a little saffron added to the soaking water.

4 steaks of tuna, or swordfish, about 7–8 oz. each, lightly scored

sea salt

extra virgin olive oil, for cooking

cilantro leaves, to serve

chermoula

a few handfuls of cilantro leaves and stems, coarsely chopped

3 garlic cloves, chopped

¼ teaspoon sweet pimentón (Spanish oak-smoked paprika)

½ teaspoon ground cumin

½ teaspoon chili powder

¼ cup extra virgin olive oil

freshly squeezed juice of ½ lemon

sea salt

a stove-top grill pan

serves 4

2 garlic cloves, chopped

1 inch fresh ginger, peeled and chopped

3 tablespoons safflower or peanut oil

4 small tomatoes, skinned and chopped

2 teaspoons white vinegar (wine or malt)

1 lb. uncooked shelled jumbo shrimp

a few curry leaves*

a few red chiles, seeded and sliced

sea salt

freshly shaved coconut, to serve

masala paste

1 small onion, quartered

grated flesh of 1/2 coconut, fresh
or frozen

2 black peppercorns

2 red chiles, seeded

1/4 teaspoon ground turmeric

2 teaspoons ground coriander

1/2 teaspoon black mustard seeds

serves 4

A recipe from Kerala, the long and fertile state in India's southwest. Kerala, like most of South India, reveres the coconut, so this shrimp and coconut recipe is a good example of its fine seafood dishes. Rice and pooris (South Indian breads) are delicious served with this dish.

coconut shrimp masala

Put all the masala ingredients into a blender and work into a thick paste, adding a dash of water if necessary to let the blades run. Remove and set aside.

Put the garlic and ginger into the clean blender and grind to a paste. Alternatively, use a mortar and pestle.

Heat 2 tablespoons oil in a wok or skillet. Add the garlic and ginger paste and sauté for a few seconds. Add the masala paste and stir-fry until the paste leaves the sides of the pan, about 8–10 minutes. Add the chopped tomatoes, vinegar, salt, and 1 cup water. Bring to a boil, add the shrimp, reduce the heat, and cook for 2–3 minutes, until the shrimp turn pink. Transfer to a serving bowl.

Heat the remaining oil in a small skillet, add the curry leaves and red chiles, and sauté for about 45 seconds or so (this is called "tempering"). Pour the tempered curry leaves and chiles over the shrimp, top with shaved coconut, and serve.

*Note Curry leaves are always best fresh, and are often available in Indian or Southeast Asian markets. Fresh ones may be frozen. If absolutely necessary, dried ones may be used instead. (Note that curry leaves are not related to the gray-leaved curry plant grown in some herb gardens.)

This is similar to the popular dish Pad Thai, but drier, less sweet and omits certain key ingredients such as eggs, substituting stir-fry vegetables instead. Tiny, blindingly hot bird's eye chiles are an essential spice in Southeast Asian cuisine: if you prefer less heat, use another kind of chile or reduce the number.

stir-fried peanut shrimp
with cilantro noodles

Put the noodles into a bowl and cover with boiling water. Let soak for 4 minutes or according to the instructions on the package. Drain, return to the bowl, and cover with cold water until ready to serve. Have a kettle of boiling water ready to reheat.

Put 3 tablespoons of the oil into a nonstick wok, heat well and swirl to coat. Add the ground coriander, kaffir lime leaves, lemongrass, red chiles, and chopped scallions and stir-fry briefly. Add the garlic and stir-fry again for 20 seconds. Add the prepared vegetables, sugar, and 2 tablespoons of the fish sauce and stir-fry over medium-high heat for 1 minute.

Add the shrimp and lemon juice and stir-fry for 1 minute, then add half the ground peanuts. Mix well, add the remaining tablespoon of fish sauce, and cook for 2 more minutes or until the shrimp turn pink.

Meanwhile, drain the noodles again and return them to the bowl. Cover with boiling water, drain, and return to the bowl. Add 2 tablespoons peanut oil, toss to coat, add the cilantro, and toss again. Add the noodles to the wok, toss to coat, then serve immediately topped with cilantro, green chiles, scallions, bean sprouts, and the remaining peanuts.

*Note You can also substitute your own choice of vegetables, such as broccoli and cauliflower florets, red bell pepper strips, asparagus tips, sliced onion, sugar snap peas, or string beans, all cut into bite-size pieces.

6 oz. rice stick noodles

5 tablespoons peanut oil

a pinch of ground coriander

2 kaffir lime leaves, 1 finely sliced or crushed and 1 left whole

1 stalk of lemongrass, very finely chopped

3–4 red bird's eye chiles, seeded and thinly sliced

3 scallions, chopped

1 large garlic clove, crushed

2 cups prepared stir-fry vegetables, without bean sprouts*

a pinch of sugar

3 tablespoons Thai fish sauce

8 oz. uncooked, shelled jumbo shrimp, deveined (about 14 oz., with shell on)

freshly squeezed juice of 1 lemon

1 cup dry-roasted peanuts, coarsely ground

¾ cup finely chopped cilantro

to serve

a handful of cilantro leaves, chopped

a few green bird's eye chiles, seeded and thinly sliced

2 scallions, green part only, thinly sliced

a handful of bean sprouts

serves 4

1 lb. firm fish such as salmon, monkfish, or cod

1 tablespoon ground turmeric

1 teaspoon salt

⅓ cup ghee (clarified butter), butter, canola, or safflower oil

1 onion, chopped

1 garlic clove, crushed

2 small green chiles, seeded if preferred, and chopped

1 inch fresh ginger, peeled and grated

12 cardamom pods, crushed

6 cloves, crushed

1 cinnamon stick, about 2 inches

2 cups canned coconut milk

freshly squeezed lemon juice, to taste

torn cilantro leaves, to serve

serves 4

A mollee is a South Indian sauce, one of those dishes known wrongly in the rest of the world as a "curry." It is mostly used for poaching fish, but is also delicious as a medium for reheating cooked meats or vegetables. The first step is to make the sauce: after that, you may add what you like. In the south of India, this is often served with great mounds of fluffy rice flavored with cumin seed.

fish mollee

Cut the fish into 1 inch strips. Mix the turmeric and salt on a plate, roll the fish in the mixture, and set aside for a few minutes.

Meanwhile, heat the ghee, butter, or oil in a flameproof casserole or large saucepan. Add the onion, garlic, chiles, ginger, cardamom, cloves, and cinnamon stick and sauté until the onion is softened and translucent.

Add the coconut milk, heat until simmering, and cook until the mixture is quite thick. Add the fish to the casserole, then spoon the sauce over the top, making sure the fish is well covered. Cook for 10 minutes on top of the stove or in a preheated oven at 300°F, until the fish is opaque all the way through. Serve sprinkled with lemon juice and cilantro.

Kerala, on the southwest coast of India, is coconut country—and one of the great spice-producing areas of the world (it was famous as such even in ancient times). The region has an inspired touch with seafood.

kerala coconut chili shrimp

Bring a large saucepan of water to a boil and plunge in the spinach for 20 seconds. Remove with a slotted spoon and refresh under cold running water to stop the cooking process; squeeze out as much water as possible. Set aside. Add the beans and cook just until crunchy, about 3 minutes. Drain, refresh in cold water, drain again, and add to the spinach.

Preheat the oven to 300°F. Heat the ghee or oil in an ovenproof casserole, add the onion, garlic, ginger, and chiles, and sauté until soft. Add the cumin, pepper, cardamom, cloves, salt, and 1 teaspoon of the lemon juice and cook for 5 minutes.

Stir in the coconut milk. Add the beans and shrimp, then stir in the chopped cilantro and the rest of the lemon juice. Cook in the preheated oven for about 25 minutes, or until the shrimp have just become opaque. Add the spinach for the last 5 minutes to reheat. Do not overcook or the shrimp will be tough.

Sprinkle with the sliced green chiles and a handful of cilantro leaves if you like, then serve with plain rice or rice mixed with pan-toasted cumin seeds.

2 cups spinach, well washed

1 cup green beans

3 tablespoons ghee (clarified butter) or peanut oil

2 onions, chopped

3 garlic cloves, chopped

1 inch fresh ginger, peeled and chopped

2 green chiles, seeded and chopped

1 tablespoon ground cumin

1 teaspoon freshly ground black pepper

6 green cardamom pods, crushed

2 cloves

a pinch of salt

freshly squeezed juice of ½ lemon

2 cups thick coconut milk

1 lb. uncooked shrimp, peeled

3 tablespoons chopped cilantro

to serve (optional)

3–4 green chiles, sliced

a handful of cilantro leaves

serves 4

1 tablespoon peanut oil

1¾ cups canned coconut milk

1½ lb. fish fillets, such as monkfish, cod, or other firm fish

spice paste

1 onion, sliced

3 garlic cloves, chopped

6 small hot green chiles, seeded and sliced

2 inches fresh ginger, peeled and sliced

1 teaspoon ground white pepper

1 teaspoon ground coriander

½ teaspoon ground turmeric

½ teaspoon ground cumin

1 teaspoon shrimp paste (see note page 77)

1 tablespoon Thai fish sauce

1 stalk of lemongrass, peeled and thinly sliced

to serve

sprigs of Thai basil (optional)*

2 limes, halved

serves 4

Thai curries are easy to make, quick to cook, and totally delicious. The secret is in the mixture of spices and the freshness of the paste. Here the paste is made in a food processor using ground spices but, if you prefer using whole ones, break them down in a coffee grinder kept solely for that purpose.

thai green fish curry

Put all the spice paste ingredients in a food processor and work them into a fine purée. Alternatively, use a mortar and pestle. Set aside.

Put the oil in a wok and heat well. Add the spice paste and stir-fry for a few seconds to release the aromas. Add the thick portion from the top of the coconut milk, stir well, and boil to thicken a little.

Add the fish and turn the pieces over in the sauce until well coated. Reheat to simmering and cook just until they start to become opaque, about 2 minutes.

Add the remaining coconut milk and continue cooking until the fish is cooked through. Serve topped with Thai basil, if using, plus the halved limes and some fragrant Thai rice or noodles.

Note Thai and Vietnamese basil is quite different from ordinary basil. It is sold in Asian food markets—omit it if you can't find it.

½ tablespoon grated fresh ginger

2 tablespoons chopped cilantro

1 teaspoon ground cumin

1 teaspoon ground coriander

1 tablespoon freshly squeezed lemon juice

4 skinless salmon fillets, 4 oz. each

1 teaspoon safflower oil

sea salt and freshly ground black pepper

dhal

1 cup red lentils, rinsed

1 onion, finely chopped

1 tablespoon grated fresh ginger

½ teaspoon ground turmeric

2 garlic cloves, sliced

1 teaspoon cumin seeds

½ teaspoon black mustard seeds

2 teaspoons safflower oil

14 oz. canned chickpeas, drained and rinsed

3 tomatoes, seeded and chopped

1½ cups baby spinach, rinsed

1 tablespoon freshly squeezed lemon juice

serves 4

A delicious dish fusing Indian dhal and spices with seared salmon, packed with health-enhancing fish oils. It's a complete meal in one and doesn't need anything else to accompany it.

spiced salmon with chickpea dhal

Start by making the spice paste for the salmon. In a bowl, mix the ginger with the cilantro, spices, lemon juice, and seasoning, then rub into the salmon fillets. Cover and set aside at room temperature to allow the flavors to develop while making the dhal.

Put the lentils in a saucepan with the onion, ginger, turmeric, and 2 cups of water and cook, covered, for 15 minutes until the lentils start to break up.

Fry the garlic, cumin seeds, and black mustard seeds in the safflower oil in a skillet until the garlic is golden and the seeds begin to pop. Quickly stir into the lentils, followed by the chickpeas. Simmer for 3 minutes.

Heat a nonstick skillet and drizzle the safflower oil over the salmon fillets. Fry the salmon for 3 minutes on each side, until the spice crust is golden and the salmon is just cooked through, but still moist.

Stir the tomatoes, spinach, and lemon juice into the dhal until the spinach has just wilted. Add seasoning to taste, then ladle the dhal onto deep plates. Place the salmon on top of the dhal to serve.

This quick curry will fill your kitchen with a wonderful aroma as it cooks. The many spices give a complex flavor to a sauce that is made in a matter of minutes.

goan shrimp curry

Mix the spices to a paste with a little water in a saucepan. Stir in the garlic, ginger, and 1⅔ cups of cold water, add seasoning, and bring to a boil. Simmer for 10 minutes until the sauce has slightly reduced and the raw flavor of the spices is released.

Meanwhile, cook the green beans in a separate saucepan of lightly salted boiling water for about 5 minutes or until tender, then drain.

Stir the tamarind concentrate and coconut milk into the spicy sauce base until smooth. Add the shrimp and cook for about 2 minutes or until they turn pink. Stir in the green beans and spinach and cook briefly until the spinach has wilted. Ladle the curry into bowls and serve with basmati rice or chapattis.

1 tablespoon ground coriander

½ tablespoon paprika

1 teaspoon ground cumin

½ teaspoon cayenne or hot chili powder

½ teaspoon ground turmeric

3 garlic cloves, crushed

2 teaspoons grated fresh ginger

8 oz. green beans, halved

1 tablespoon tamarind concentrate or freshly squeezed lemon juice

2 tablespoons canned coconut milk

14 oz. uncooked tiger shrimp, shelled and deveined

3½ oz. baby spinach, rinsed

sea salt and freshly ground black pepper

serves 4

Green curry is a staple dish of Thailand. The green curry paste here will make 6–10 tablespoons of paste. Freeze the leftovers in ice cube trays, then decant the cubes into a freezer bag. Each cube will give about 1 tablespoon paste.

green curry with shrimp

First make the green curry paste. Using a mortar and pestle, grind all the ingredients to a thick paste.

Heat the oil in a large saucepan, add the garlic, and sauté until golden brown. Stir in 2 tablespoons of the green curry paste, mixing well. Add the shrimp and stir-fry until just cooked through. Add the coconut cream and bring to a boil, stirring constantly. Add the stock. Return to a boil, stirring constantly.

Keeping the curry simmering, add the chiles, fish sauce, eggplant, and sugar and simmer until the eggplant are cooked but still crunchy (do not overcook or the shrimp will be tough).

Stir in the basil leaves just before pouring into the serving bowl. Serve with rice and other Thai dishes.

2 tablespoons peanut or safflower oil

2 garlic cloves, finely chopped

12 uncooked jumbo shrimp, shelled and deveined

2¾ cups coconut cream

2¾ cups vegetable stock

2 large red chiles, sliced diagonally into thin ovals

¼ cup Thai fish sauce

8 round green Thai eggplant, quartered, or 1 Chinese eggplant, cut into ½ inch slices

1 tablespoon sugar

30 fresh sweet basil leaves

green curry paste

1 teaspoon coriander seeds

1 teaspoon cumin seeds

1 teaspoon white peppercorns

1 tablespoon chopped lemongrass

1 inch fresh galangal or ginger, peeled and chopped

2 long green chiles, chopped

10 small green chiles, chopped

2 tablespoons chopped garlic

3 pink Thai shallots or 1 regular, chopped

3 cilantro roots, chopped

1 teaspoon finely chopped kaffir lime leaves

2 teaspoons shrimp paste (see note page 77)

serves 4

2 tablespoons peanut or safflower oil

2 garlic cloves, finely chopped

2 small red or green chiles,
finely chopped

12 uncooked jumbo shrimp, shelled and
deveined, tail on

2 medium onions, halved and
thickly sliced

3 tablespoons Thai fish sauce

2 tablespoons light soy sauce

1 teaspoon sugar

30 holy basil leaves

serves 4

This is a good dish to try if you are new to the tastes of Thai food. You will enjoy the combination of fresh shrimp with the strongly aromatic basil. It's easy to vary the amount of chile, too, in case very spicy food isn't to your taste. This is an excellent dish for the beginner cook.

shrimp with chile and basil

Heat the oil in a wok or skillet, add the garlic and chiles, and stir-fry until the garlic begins to brown. Stir in the shrimp, then add the onions, fish sauce, soy sauce, sugar, and basil, mixing well. Cook until the shrimp are cooked through (it will take just a few minutes—until the shrimp become opaque). Transfer to a dish and serve with other Thai dishes, including rice.

Variations Instead of shrimp, use 1 lb. of pork, beef, or chicken, all finely chopped or ground. In Thailand, the shrimp would also be chopped or ground, but in the West, whole shrimp are used instead.

Thai curry is a great flavor hit when you get in from a busy day. This recipe uses a ready-made paste to make everything easier, but your curry will only be as good as your paste. Thai brands are always good, but remember that they are often very hot.

red curry
with shrimp and pumpkin

If you remember, put the coconut milk in the refrigerator as soon as you buy it.

When you are ready to start cooking, scrape off the thick coconut cream that usually clings to the lid and put just the cream in a wok or large saucepan over medium heat. Add the curry paste and stir for 1–2 minutes until the paste smells fragrant, then add the sugar and cook for a further 2 minutes until sticky.

Pour in the rest of the coconut milk, add the lemongrass, pumpkin, and $1/3$–$1/2$ cup water to almost cover the pumpkin. Bring the contents of the wok to a gentle simmer and let bubble away gently for 10 minutes, or until the pumpkin is tender.

Add the sugar snap peas and cook for 2 minutes, then add the shrimp and cook for a further 2 minutes or until they turn pink. Remove from the heat and stir in the fish sauce. Transfer to bowls and sprinkle with the mint and chile. Taste and add more fish sauce if necessary. Serve with steamed jasmine rice.

14 oz. canned coconut milk

2 tablespoons Thai red curry paste

2 tablespoons palm sugar
or natural cane sugar

1 lemongrass stalk, cut in half
and bruised

14 oz. pie pumpkin or butternut
squash, peeled, seeded, and cut
into 1 inch chunks

4 oz. sugar snap peas, cut diagonally

$6^{1}/_{2}$ oz. uncooked tiger shrimp, shelled,
deveined, and butterflied but tails intact

2 tablespoons Thai fish sauce, plus extra
to taste

15 mint leaves, finely shredded

1 large red chile, seeded and cut into
thin strips

serves 4

"Tartare" means uncooked and, to serve fish this way, you must use very fresh, sashimi-grade tuna. If you prefer your tuna cooked, sear the whole steak on a preheated stove-top grill pan for 1 minute on each side or until cooked to your liking. However, I do urge you to try it tartare—it is delicious, as the Japanese well know.

chili tuna tartare pasta

Cook the pasta according to the instructions on the package.

Meanwhile, heat the oil in a skillet, add the garlic, and sauté gently for 2 minutes until lightly golden. Add the chile, lemon zest, and thyme and sauté for a further 1 minute.

Drain the pasta, reserving ¼ cup of the cooking liquid, and return both to the pan. Stir in the hot garlic oil mixture, the lemon juice, the raw tuna, basil leaves, salt, and pepper, and a little extra olive oil. Serve at once.

12 oz. dried fusilli or other pasta

⅓ cup extra virgin olive oil

4 garlic cloves, sliced

1–2 dried red chiles, seeded and chopped

grated zest and juice of 1 unwaxed lemon

1 tablespoon chopped thyme leaves

1 lb. tuna steak, chopped

a handful of basil leaves

sea salt and freshly ground black pepper

serves 4

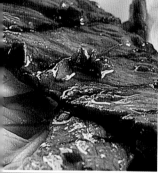

meat dishes

Choose lean pork chops for this dish and trim off any excess fat. The spicy marinade, which makes the chops ideal for broiling, can also be brushed onto chicken breasts and other meats. Begin cooking the potatoes before you cook the pork, but don't add the peas and yogurt until just before serving.

indian grilled pork chops
with spiced potatoes and peas

1 tablespoon Madras curry paste

2 tablespoons mango chutney

½ teaspoon ground turmeric

2 tablespoons safflower oil

4 loin pork chops (each weighing about 5 oz.)

5 oz. cherry tomatoes, on the vine if available

sea salt and freshly ground black pepper

spiced potatoes and peas

1¾ lb. potatoes, such as Yukon gold, peeled and diced

1 tablespoon safflower oil

2 tablespoons unsalted butter

1 onion, finely chopped

1 garlic clove, crushed

1 teaspoon cumin seeds

1 cup baby peas (fresh or frozen)

2 tablespoons Greek yogurt

sea salt

serves 4

First make the spiced potatoes. Cook the potatoes for 10 minutes in a pan of boiling salted water. Drain in a colander. Heat the oil and butter in a skillet and add the onion, garlic, and cumin seeds. Cook over low heat until the onions have softened. Add the potatoes and ½ cup water, and continue to cook until the potatoes are tender, for a further 10 minutes.

Meanwhile, preheat the broiler. Put the curry paste, mango chutney, turmeric, and 1 tablespoon oil in a bowl and mix well with salt and pepper. Put the chops on a broiler, season well with salt and pepper, and brush with half the curry mixture. Arrange the cherry tomatoes on the broiler rack alongside the pork and drizzle with the remaining oil.

Cook the chops and tomatoes under the preheated broiler for 5–6 minutes or until the pork is slightly charred. Brush the other side with the remaining curry mixture and cook for a further 5–6 minutes.

Add the peas and yogurt to the potatoes just before you are about to serve. Bring to a boil and let bubble for 1 minute.

To serve, put a few generous spoonfuls of the spiced potatoes and peas on each warmed serving plate and place a pork chop on top along with some tomatoes, still attached to their vine if possible.

Since your friends can help themselves and put together their own traditional fajitas, this dish is straightforward to serve. If you prefer a very spicy guacamole, add a couple of extra jalapeño chiles, seeded and finely chopped.

4 small sirloin steaks, about 1 inch thick (each weighing about 6 oz.)

4 tablespoons extra virgin olive oil

1 tablespoon pimentón (Spanish oak-smoked paprika)

1 tablespoon cumin

2 ripe Haas avocados, peeled and pitted

freshly squeezed juice of 1 lime

1 small white onion, finely grated

1 large red onion, cut into petals

1 red or green bell pepper, cored, seeded, and thinly sliced

3 garlic cloves, cut into slivers

8–12 wheat or corn flour tortillas

sea salt and freshly ground black pepper

to serve

2–3 jalapeño chiles, seeded and chopped

a handful of arugula leaves

sour cream

salsa

a stove-top grill pan (optional)

serves 4–6

stir-fried beef fajitas
with guacamole and sour cream

Preheat the oven to 325°F.

Remove any fat from the beef and cut it diagonally, across the grain, to create finger-length strips. Mix together 2 tablespoons of the olive oil, the pimentón, and cumin in a large bowl. Add the beef pieces and toss until evenly coated in the spiced oil. Set aside while you prepare the guacamole and onions and peppers.

To make the guacamole, roughly mash the avocados in a bowl, leaving some lumps, and stir in the lime juice and white onion. Set aside until needed.

Heat a heavy-based stove-top grill pan or large frying pan over a high heat with the remaining oil and stir-fry the red onion, bell pepper, and garlic for 3–4 minutes, until they start to go limp and the edges begin to char. Remove from the pan and set aside in a warm place.

Wrap the tortillas in foil and place them in the preheated oven to warm, for about 5 minutes. (Alternatively, you can follow the package instructions for warming them in the microwave.)

Meanwhile, wipe the grill pan clean with paper towels. Heat until smoking hot, then drop the strips of meat into the pan over high heat, working in batches and turning them frequently. Each batch should take no more than 1–2 minutes to cook. Season the meat with salt and pepper.

To serve, arrange the beef strips, guacamole, bell peppers and onion, jalapeño chiles, arugula, sour cream, and salsa, if using, in separate bowls. Wrap the tortillas in a cloth napkin, put them in a basket or dish (so that they don't dry out and get hard), and bring them to the table. Let everyone dig in.

4 sirloin or T-bone steaks

olive oil, for brushing

sea salt and freshly ground black pepper

chimichurri parsley base

3 cups fresh flat-leaf parsley, trimmed of tough stalks and coarsely chopped

2 large garlic cloves, quartered

½ teaspoon sweet pimentón (Spanish oak-smoked paprika)

¼ teaspoon freshly grated nutmeg

a pinch of ground cinnamon

a pinch of chili powder or hot red pepper flakes

2 tablespoons freshly squeezed lemon juice

½ cup extra virgin olive oil or corn oil

sea salt, to taste

chimichurri dressing

½ small onion, finely chopped

¾ teaspoon superfine sugar

1 teaspoon freshly squeezed lemon juice

1 red bell pepper, finely chopped (about ⅓ cup)

¼ teaspoon freshly grated nutmeg

2 tablespoons extra virgin olive oil or corn oil

serves 4

Argentine beef is legendary, thanks to the plentiful grazing land of the pampas and the country's cowboys, the gauchos. Beef is often cooked on a parrilla—a large grill—and served on its own or with condiments like chimichurri. Serve the steaks with grilled vegetables and baked potatoes, which can be cooked in the coals.

argentine grilled beef with chimichurri

To make the chimichurri parsley base, put all the ingredients into a blender and work to a smooth sauce. Alternatively, use a mortar and pestle.

Next make the dressing. Put the chopped onion into a bowl, add the sugar and lemon juice, and stir well. Cover and set aside for at least 30 minutes. Add the red pepper, nutmeg, oil, and 3–4 tablespoons of the chimichurri parsley base. Mix well and set aside. (Save any remaining chimichurri base for use as a pesto-type topping, or pour into ice cube trays, freeze, and use for flavoring stocks, soups, and stews.)

To prepare the beef, preheat a charcoal grill until very hot (you can add oak or hickory chips if available) and brush the steaks with a little oil. Cook over high heat to begin with, then adjust the rack further away from the fire as soon as the surfaces of the steaks have begun to sear. Cook to your liking, turning once during cooking. Alternatively, cook under a preheated broiler or on a stove-top grill pan. Sprinkle with salt and pepper and serve hot with the chimichurri.

Variation Finely chop 1 poblano or other mild green chile and mix with the chimichurri.

2 tablespoons unsalted butter or ghee (clarified butter)

5 green cardamom pods, bruised

½ cinnamon stick

2½ lb. leg of lamb, well trimmed, boned, and cut into chunks, or 1¾ lb. boned

⅓ cup plain yogurt, beaten

¼ teaspoon cardamom seeds (not pods)

1½ cups heavy cream

sea salt

wet paste

2 large garlic cloves, sliced

1½ large onions, quartered

4 green chiles, seeded and coarsely chopped

⅓ cup ground almonds

to serve

freshly ground white pepper

finely sliced red onion, soaked in a little vinegar

unroasted slivered almonds

serves 4–6

Rich and creamy and steeped in plenty of almond and cardamom sauce, this "white" dish is a refined affair. The wet paste of garlic, chiles, almonds, and onions provides body and a flavor typical of northern India, while the cardamom and cinnamon scent the butter or ghee before other ingredients are added. White pepper is classically used in this dish, in keeping with its color.

spicy lamb in almond milk

To make the wet paste, put the garlic, onions, chiles, and almonds into a blender and blend until smooth, adding a little water to let the blades run. Alternatively, use a mortar and pestle. Set aside.

Melt the butter or ghee in a large, heavy saucepan and add the cardamom pods and cinnamon stick. Let the spices flavor the butter for 1–2 minutes, then add the wet paste. Sauté the paste for 8 minutes until thickened, stirring frequently to avoid burning.

Add the lamb and stir-fry until brown. Then add the yogurt and enough water to cover, about 1–1½ cups. Beat well. Heat until almost boiling, stirring constantly. Partly cover with a lid, reduce the heat to low, and simmer very gently for 45 minutes. (Lamb cooked over low heat becomes very tender.)

Remove the lid, then stir in the cardamom seeds and salt. Cook for 30 minutes longer. The sauce may look slightly separated, but don't worry.

Finally, stir in the cream, increase the heat, and bring to a boil. Reduce the heat and simmer gently for a few minutes to let the sauce thicken slightly. Sprinkle with white pepper, sliced red onion, and a few slivered almonds. Serve with boiled rice and naan bread.

1 large boneless sirloin steak, 1–1½ inches thick, about 1 lb., trimmed of fat

2 tablespoons tamari or other soy sauce

1 teaspoon toasted sesame oil

1–2 teaspoons sugar

1 garlic clove, crushed

1 inch fresh ginger, peeled and finely grated

2 scallions, trimmed and chopped

1–2 bird's eye chiles, red or green, seeded and chopped

a pinch of salt

lettuce leaves, to serve

a stove-top grill pan (optional)

serves 4

This is a Korean delight—as popular with tourists as it is with the locals. Bulgogi is an appetizer that can be made and served in two ways. The beef strips, always sliced very thinly, can be wide or narrow. The wide ones are served with rice and condiments, while the narrow ones, as here, are rolled up in lettuce leaves—an entirely satisfying way of eating this dish.

bulgogi

Freeze the steak for 1 hour so it will be easy to slice very thinly. Remove the steak from the freezer, then slice very thinly crosswise.

To make the marinade, put the tamari or soy, sesame oil, and sugar into a bowl and beat well. Stir in the garlic, ginger, scallions, chiles, and salt, then add the beef strips, mix well to coat, cover, and refrigerate for several hours to develop the flavors.

Heat a lightly greased stove-top grill pan or skillet until very hot. Sear the strips of steak briefly on both sides until just done, working in batches so you don't overcrowd the pan. Either pile onto a large plate or divide between 4 plates, and serve with lettuce.

¾ cup raw peanuts

1¾ lb. cubed steak

1¼ teaspoons tamarind concentrate

2 cans coconut milk, 14 oz. each

1 large potato, chopped into
large chunks

sea salt or fish sauce

mussaman spice paste

2 cardamom pods

½ cinnamon stick

1 teaspoon cumin seeds

1½ tablespoons coriander seeds

½ teaspoon freshly grated nutmeg

5 red bird's eye chiles, seeded
and chopped

1 stalk of lemongrass, very
finely chopped

4 garlic cloves, chopped

4 small Thai shallots, coarsely chopped

3 tablespoons chopped cilantro
stems or roots

a tiny piece of shrimp paste, toasted,
(see note page 77), or 1 teaspoon
anchovy paste

serves 6

This unusual Thai curry is characterized by its thick peanut sauce and it is a firm favorite, inside and outside Thailand. As it is exceedingly rich, serve in smaller portions than you would usually.

thai mussaman beef curry

Put the peanuts in a dry skillet and toast until aromatic. Transfer to a clean dish towel and rub together. Their skins should slip off easily. Using a mortar and pestle or food processor, grind the peanuts coarsely and set aside.

Put the beef into a large, heavy saucepan, add 2 cups water and bring to a boil. Reduce the heat and simmer for about 1½ hours, then add sea salt or fish sauce, to taste.

To make the spice paste, put the cardamom, cinnamon, cumin seeds, and coriander seeds in a dry skillet and toast until aromatic. Using a blender or mortar and pestle, grind to a fine powder. Add the nutmeg, chiles, lemongrass, garlic, shallots, cilantro stems, and shrimp paste and grind to a thick paste, adding a little water if necessary.

Remove the beef from the saucepan and set aside. The liquid will be substantially reduced, so take care not to let the dish burn at this last stage. You should stir frequently and keep the heat low.

Add the tamarind and half the spice paste and stir. (Freeze the remaining paste for future use.) Stir the coconut milk into the sauce. Return the beef to the saucepan, then add the potatoes—if the mixture is looking too dry, add a little extra water. Simmer gently for 20 minutes, stirring frequently. Stir in the peanuts and cook for another 1–2 minutes. Serve with rice.

3 tablespoons peanut or safflower oil

1½ lb. well trimmed boneless sparerib, sliced into chunks*

2 cups beef stock

hinleh (curry) paste

4–6 red bird's eye chiles, seeded and chopped

5 garlic cloves, quartered

½ onion, coarsely chopped

2 inches fresh ginger, peeled and grated

¼ teaspoon ground turmeric

2 inches fresh galangal, peeled and grated

1 stalk of lemongrass, very finely chopped

3 anchovies in oil, drained and finely chopped plus a dash of fish sauce, or ½ teaspoon dried shrimp paste, toasted (see note, page 77)

to serve

a handful of Thai basil or cilantro

2 red bird's eye chiles, thinly sliced lengthwise

serves 4

This hinleh (curry) is a Burmese specialty and doesn't include the coconut milk so typical of Southeast Asian cooking. It does use three root spices from the same family—turmeric, ginger, and galangal. If you can't get fresh galangal, use extra fresh ginger instead.

burmese pork hinleh

To make the hinleh paste, put all the ingredients into a blender and grind to a paste, adding a dash of water to let the blades run. Alternatively, use a mortar and pestle.

Heat the oil in a large saucepan and add the paste. Stir-fry for several minutes. Add the pork and stir-fry to seal. Add the stock, bring to a boil, reduce the heat, and simmer gently, stirring occasionally, for 40–45 minutes until cooked through but very tender. Sprinkle with the herbs and chile and serve with rice.

*Note Boneless sparerib meat takes longer to cook than leg meat, but doesn't dry out as easily. It gives best results at a lower temperature. Otherwise, you can also use the best cut—filet or tenderloin—for tender, fast-cooking meat.

This Texan classic is justly world famous. Chili con Carne is almost always made with chili powder, but it is also good made with crushed dried chiles or sliced fresh ones. For timid tastebuds, adjust the quantity of chiles or chili powder to suit.

chili con carne

2½ cups dried red kidney beans, washed

½ teaspoon salt

2 tablespoons shortening, corn oil, or beef drippings

2 onions, sliced

3 garlic cloves, sliced

2 lb. beef chuck, cut into ½-inch cubes

2 tablespoons all-purpose flour

2 tablespoons tomato paste

¼–½ tablespoon chili powder, dried chili flakes, or 1–4 whole red serrano chiles, seeded if preferred, then chopped

1 green bell pepper, seeded and chopped

¼ teaspoon ground cumin

4 cups beef stock

salt, to taste

to serve

a little chopped cilantro

sour cream (optional)

Put the beans in a bowl, cover with cold water, and let soak for at least 3 hours or overnight. (If short of time, put them in a saucepan, cover with cold water, bring to a boil, simmer for 2 minutes, remove from the heat, cover, and let soak for 1 hour.) When ready to cook, drain, then rinse in cold water.

Put the beans in a saucepan, cover with cold water, bring to a boil, and boil hard for 15 minutes. Drain, cover with fresh water, and return to a boil. Simmer for 1–4 hours or until tender (the time depends on the age of the beans): top up with boiling water as necessary. Add ½ teaspoon salt 15 minutes before the end of cooking. Set aside.

Put the shortening, oil, or drippings in a large skillet and heat until melted. Add the onion and garlic and cook gently until softened and lightly browned, about 15 minutes. Transfer to a plate and keep them warm.

Add the beef cubes to the skillet, in batches if necessary—do not crowd the pan. Sauté until browned on all sides. Stir in the flour and mix well. Add the tomato paste, chili powder, bell pepper, cumin, and stock and strain in any cooking liquid from the cooked beans. Bring to a boil, transfer to a flameproof casserole dish or saucepan, and simmer on top of the stove or in a preheated oven at 300°F for 1¼ hours, or until the meat is tender.

Remove from the heat or oven, season to taste, stir in the beans, return to the stove top or oven, and cook for a further 30 minutes.

Sprinkle with chopped cilantro and top with a spoonful of sour cream, if using. Serve with warmed tortillas or rice.

The biryani is especially popular in North India and Pakistan. It often includes lamb, although chicken is used here. For celebrations, it may have gold or silver leaf on top.

saffron and pistachio biryani

Put the saffron into a large saucepan with ⅔ cup water and ½ teaspoon of the salt. Bring to a boil, then set aside to cool.

Melt 6 tablespoons of the butter in a second saucepan. Add the rice and sauté gently, stirring continuously, until the rice is white and opaque, about 5 minutes. Add 4 cups water, 1 teaspoon salt, 1 cinnamon stick, 3 cloves, 1 bay leaf, and half the cardamom. Cover, bring to a boil, reduce the heat, and simmer until the water has been absorbed, about 10–15 minutes. (The rice will be slightly undercooked.)

Measure 2⅔ cups of this partially cooked rice and add to the pan of saffron water. Stir well, cover with a lid, bring to a boil, and cook for a couple of minutes or until the rice has absorbed all the water. Add ½ cup water to the remaining white rice, stir, cover, bring to a boil, and cook for a couple of minutes or until the rice has absorbed all the water. Measure a further 2⅔ cups of this rice and mix it gently with the saffron rice to give a yellow and white mixture. Spread the remaining white rice into an a shallow casserole dish and set aside.

Rinse out the saucepan, add the remaining butter and heat gently. Stir in the remaining cinnamon stick, cloves, bay leaf, cardamom, and the ground cumin and sauté to release the aromas.

Meanwhile, put the onion, ginger, chiles, garlic, and 5 tablespoons water in a blender and purée until smooth. Pour this mixture into the pan of hot spices and heat until the water has boiled away and the butter begins to sauté the mixture. Add the chicken and seal all over without browning it or the spices. Add the yogurt, mint, cilantro, and remaining salt and cover with a lid. Raise the heat and simmer, without boiling, for 20 minutes. (Don't worry when the sauce appears to split and become buttery.) Preheat the oven to 375°F. Remove the chicken and arrange on top of the rice in the casserole, pour the yogurt sauce over, cover, and cook in the preheated oven for 20 minutes while the rice absorbs the liquid.

Remove from the oven and arrange the bi-colored rice on top, then return for 5 minutes to heat through. Serve topped with the onion, nuts, raisins, and cilantro.

a large pinch of saffron threads

2½ teaspoons salt

1 cup butter or ghee (clarified butter)

2¾ cups basmati rice

2 cinnamon sticks

6 cloves

2 bay leaves

6 green cardamom pods, crushed

1 tablespoon ground cumin

½ onion, sliced

1 inch fresh ginger, peeled and sliced

2 red chiles, seeded and sliced

3 garlic cloves, crushed

4 chicken breasts, skinless and boneless

1 cup natural whole-milk yogurt

1 tablespoon chopped mint

1 tablespoon lightly chopped cilantro

to serve

½ onion, fried till crisp, then crumbled

½ cup green pistachio nuts, shelled, blanched, and peeled

⅓ cup almonds, toasted in a dry skillet, then sliced

⅓ cup raisins, soaked in 2 tablespoons boiling water for 30 minutes

a handful of cilantro leaves

serves 4

2 lb. leg or shoulder of lamb, boned and cubed

3 cups canned coconut milk

a handful of fresh coconut slivers or 1 tablespoon unsweetened dried shredded coconut

a handful of cilantro leaves, to serve

spicy masala paste

⅓ cup peanut oil

3 onions, chopped

2 inches fresh ginger, peeled and grated

3 large garlic cloves, chopped

1 teaspoon ground cinnamon

1 tablespoon ground cumin

1 tablespoon ground coriander

¼ teaspoon ground cardamom

1 teaspoon ground turmeric

2 teaspoons hot red pepper flakes

3 tablespoons vinegar

1 teaspoon salt

tempering

2 tablespoons mustard oil or peanut oil

2 red onions, cut into wedges

2 tablespoons mustard seeds

serves 4

This recipe can be made even richer if you have time to allow the flavors of the masala paste and lamb to consolidate overnight. This hearty lamb dish will still be delicious if you can't wait, however.

spiced lamb with coconut

To make the masala paste, heat the oil in a wok, skillet, or metal casserole dish, add the onions, ginger, and garlic, and stir-fry until lightly browned. Add the cinnamon, cumin, ground coriander, cardamom, turmeric, and pepper flakes and cook until the fragrance is released, 3–4 minutes. Stir in the vinegar and salt.

Add the lamb to the pan and sauté, turning frequently, for about 10 minutes until lightly browned on all sides. At this point, you may remove it from the heat, let cool, then chill overnight to marinate and develop the flavors (if time is short, this step may be omitted).

Add about 2⅔ cups of the coconut milk. Add water to cover, heat to simmering, then cook until the meat is tender, about 40 minutes. Stir from time to time to prevent the mixture from sticking to the pan. Stir in the rest of the coconut milk and cook for a further 10 minutes.

Meanwhile, put the coconut in a dry wok or skillet and stir-fry for a few minutes until lightly golden: take care, the pieces can easily burn. Set aside.

To make the tempering, heat the oil in a wok or skillet, add the onion and mustard seeds, and stir-fry until the onion is softened and dark golden brown around the edges. Remove from the heat.

Transfer the lamb to a serving dish, spoon the tempering over the top, and the coconut on top of that. Add the cilantro and serve with other Indian dishes.

This is a dish of contrasts. It has a mixture of different textures in the soft noodles and crunchy vegetables, plus both hot and sour flavors.

chili beef noodles

Put the noodles in a heatproof bowl, cover with boiling water and let soak for 3 minutes. Drain and refresh with cold water, then set aside.

Toss the slices of steak together with the onion, garlic, and chile. Heat the safflower oil in a nonstick skillet or wok over high heat. Add the beef mixture and stir-fry for 2 minutes. Mix in the bean sprouts and snow peas and cook, stirring, for 1 minute.

Stir the noodles into the pan with the lime juice and fish sauce and heat through. Pile into 2 serving bowls and serve immediately, topped with the chopped cilantro.

3½ oz. rice noodles

5 oz. beef rump steak, trimmed and thinly sliced

1 red onion, thinly sliced

2 garlic cloves, thinly sliced

1 red chile, seeded and thinly sliced

1 teaspoon safflower oil

1 cup bean sprouts

¾ cup snow peas, halved diagonally

1 tablespoon freshly squeezed lime juice

1 tablespoon Thai fish sauce

2 tablespoons chopped cilantro, to serve

serves 2

An easy dish to prepare and cook, this is a suitable recipe for those new to Thai cooking. The combination of garlic and chile ensures a very hot and traditional Thai flavor.

2 tablespoons peanut or safflower oil

3 large garlic cloves, finely chopped

1 lb. lean pork, thinly sliced

2 tablespoons Thai fish sauce

2 tablespoons light soy sauce

2 large red chiles, thinly sliced

sliced scallions, to serve

serves 4

pork with garlic
and fresh chile

Heat the oil in a wok or skillet until a light haze appears. Add the garlic and stir-fry until golden brown. Add the pork and stir-fry briefly.

Add the fish sauce, soy sauce, and chiles, stirring briefly all the time. By now the pork should be cooked through. Spoon onto a serving dish and top with sliced scallions. Serve with 3–4 other Thai dishes, including rice, noodles, and perhaps fresh pickle.

Variations Instead of the pork, use a similar quantity of thinly sliced chicken or beef, or shelled and deveined shrimp.

8 large or 12 medium lamb chops, trimmed of fat

2 tablespoons extra virgin olive oil, plus extra to drizzle

1 teaspoon cumin seeds

two 14 oz. cans chickpeas, drained

10 oz. cherry tomatoes, on the vine

¼ cup chopped cilantro

sea salt and freshly ground black pepper

marinade

2 tablespoons extra virgin olive oil

2 tablespoons chopped mint

finely grated peel of 1 unwaxed lemon

5 tablespoons freshly squeezed lemon juice

1 teaspoon ground red pepper

1 garlic clove, peeled and crushed

serves 4

The lemony, minty marinade is perfect here with lamb chops that are grilled to rosy perfection. The marinade is also very good with chicken, shrimp, and fish. Mashing the chickpeas by hand produces a less gluey result than using a food processor.

cumin-spiced lamb chops with chickpea mash and roasted vine tomatoes

To make the marinade, combine the olive oil, mint, lemon peel, and 1 tablespoon of juice, the ground red pepper, and garlic in a large bowl. Add the lamb chops, season well, and toss. If you have time, marinate for an hour; if not, move on.

Heat ½ tablespoon of the olive oil in a skillet over medium heat, add the cumin seeds and stir for 30 seconds until fragrant. Tip in the chickpeas and toss in the oil for 1 minute. Stir in the remaining lemon juice and ⅓ cup water, cover, and simmer for 10 minutes until softened. Preheat the broiler to high.

Put the lamb chops on a baking sheet lined with aluminum foil and broil for 5–6 minutes until blackened around the edges. Turn over, add the tomatoes (halving any large ones), drizzle with the remaining olive oil, season, and broil for a further 5–6 minutes.

Mash the chickpeas with a potato masher until you get a chunky purée. Add the cilantro, season to taste, and stir. Transfer to bowls and top with 2 or 3 lamb chops. Drizzle with olive oil and lamb juices.

3 lemongrass stalks

7 oz. ground lamb

2 shallots, finely chopped

2 teaspoons chopped parsley

2 teaspoons chopped cilantro

½ teaspoon ground allspice

1 small red chile, seeded and
finely chopped

flour, for dusting

2 tablespoons sunflower oil

½ small red bell pepper, seeded and
cut into thin strips

12 white mini pita, warmed

12 crisp baby lettuce leaves

12 small sprigs cilantro

minted cream

½ cup crème fraîche or sour cream

2 tablespoons mint, chopped

salt and freshly ground black pepper

serves 4 (makes 12)

These fragrant mini-kabobs are popular in Morocco and Tunisia. The lemongrass skewers add a fragrance and opulence to the koftas, but you can use pre-soaked wooden toothpicks if preferred.

lamb kofta wraps
with minted cream

Slice the lemongrass in half widthwise, then lengthwise to make 12 sticks. In a bowl, mix the ground lamb, shallots, parsley, cilantro, allspice, and chile together. Divide into twelve and with lightly floured hands shape into 2 inch long finger shapes. Thread the koftas onto the lemongrass skewers.

In a small bowl mix the crème fraîche and mint together and season with salt and freshly ground black pepper.

Heat the oil in a skillet and fry the koftas for 4–5 minutes, turning to brown on all sides. At the same time add the pepper strips and cook for 3–4 minutes, to soften and brown slightly.

Open each pita bread lengthwise, place a lettuce leaf in each, and add a kofta, a few strips of red pepper, and a sprig of cilantro. Serve with the minted cream.

These Moroccan-inspired wraps are perfect for an informal lunch. Serve the kabobs, a dish of couscous, and a pile of chapatti wraps and invite your guests to help themselves.

lamb and couscous wraps
with harissa dressing

In a shallow dish mix 2 tablespoons of the olive oil, the lemon juice, coriander, turmeric, and harissa paste together. Cut the lamb into chunks, add to the dish, toss to coat, cover, and let marinate in a cool place for 30 minutes or longer, if time allows. Next make the harissa dressing: in a small bowl, mix together the yogurt, harissa paste, and cilantro and season with salt and pepper.

Preheat the broiler to medium. Thread the chunks of lamb onto the skewers with the onion wedges. Place on a broiler rack and brush with the remaining marinade. Put the couscous in a saucepan, pour over the hot broth, cover, and let stand for 10 minutes, stirring occasionally.

Put the kabobs under the preheated broiler and cook for 8–10 minutes, until browned on the outside but pink in the center.

Warm the chapattis in a microwave oven for 1–1½ minutes, or in a warm oven, wrapped in foil. Heat the couscous for 1–2 minutes to warm through, if necessary. Stir in the remaining olive oil, the scallions, apricots, lemons (if using), almonds, and cilantro.

Either serve the warm chapattis with the kabobs, couscous, and dressing separately, or assemble first by topping each chapatti with a little couscous, then the meat and onions from a kabob. Drizzle the dressing over, before rolling up and securing with a toothpick if wished.

3 tablespoons olive oil

1 teaspoon freshly squeezed lemon juice

1 teaspoon ground coriander

½ teaspoon ground turmeric

1 teaspoon harissa paste

1¼ pounds lean lamb from the leg

2 small red onions, each cut into 8 wedges

1 cup couscous

¾ cup boiling vegetable broth

8 chapattis

4 scallions, shredded

8 dried apricots, chopped

2 miniature preserved lemons, thinly sliced (optional)

3 tablespoons toasted flaked almonds

1 tablespoon chopped cilantro

harissa dressing

⅔ cup plain yogurt

2 teaspoons harissa paste

1 tablespoon chopped cilantro

salt and freshly ground black pepper

8 wooden skewers, soaked in water for 30 minutes

toothpicks (optional)

serves 4 (makes 8)

Tagines made with meatballs (kefta) do not require long cooking. Generally, the sauce is prepared first and the meatballs are poached in it, until just cooked. This popular meatball recipe is light and lemony and is delicious served with a salad and couscous tossed with chile and herbs.

tagine of spicy kefta
with lemon

To make the kefta, pound the ground meat with your knuckles in a bowl. Using your hands, lift up the lump of ground meat and slap it back down into the bowl. Add the onion, parsley, cinnamon, cumin, coriander, and cayenne, and season to taste with salt and black pepper. Using your hands, mix the ingredients together and knead well, pounding the mixture for a few minutes. Take pieces of the mixture and shape them into little walnut-size balls, so that you end up with about 16 kefta. (These can be made ahead of time and kept in the refrigerator for 2–3 days.)

Heat the oil and butter together in a tagine or heavy-based casserole dish. Stir in the onion, garlic, ginger, and chile and sauté until they begin to brown. Add the turmeric and half the cilantro and mint, and pour in roughly 1¼ cups water. Bring the water to a boil, reduce the heat, and simmer, covered, for 10 minutes. Carefully place the kefta in the liquid, cover, and poach the kefta for about 15 minutes, rolling them in the liquid from time to time so they are cooked well on all sides. Pour over the lemon juice, season the liquid with salt, and tuck the lemon segments around the kefta. Poach for a further 10 minutes.

Sprinkle with the remaining cilantro and mint and serve hot.

1 tablespoon olive oil

1 tablespoon butter or ghee (clarified butter)

1 onion, roughly chopped

2–3 garlic cloves, halved and crushed

a thumb-size piece of fresh ginger, peeled and finely chopped

1 red chile, thinly sliced

2 teaspoons ground turmeric

a small bunch of cilantro, roughly chopped

a small bunch of mint, chopped

freshly squeezed juice of 1 lemon

1 lemon, cut into 4 or 6 segments, with pips removed

kefta

1 lb. finely ground beef or lamb

1 onion, finely chopped or grated

a small bunch of flat leaf parsley, finely chopped

1–2 teaspoons ground cinnamon

1 teaspoon ground cumin

1 teaspoon ground coriander

½ teaspoon cayenne pepper, or 1 teaspoon paprika

sea salt and freshly ground black pepper

a tagine (optional)

serves 4–6

1 lemongrass stalk

1¼ lb. ground pork

⅓ cup breadcrumbs

6 kaffir lime leaves, very thinly sliced

2 garlic cloves, crushed

1 inch fresh ginger, grated

1 red chile, seeded and chopped

2 tablespoons Thai fish sauce

to serve

lettuce leaves

a handful of herb leaves such as mint, cilantro, and Thai basil

sweet chili sauce

4 wooden skewers soaked in cold water for 30 minutes

serves 4

Like many Vietnamese dishes, these delicious pork balls are served wrapped in a lettuce leaf with plenty of fresh herbs and sweet chili sauce.

vietnamese pork balls

Using a sharp knife, trim the lemongrass stalk to about 6 inches, then remove and discard the tough outer leaves. Chop the inner stalk very finely.

Put the ground pork and breadcrumbs in a bowl, add the lemongrass, lime leaves, garlic, ginger, chile, and fish sauce and mix well. Let marinate in the refrigerator for at least 1 hour.

Using your hands, shape the mixture into 20 small balls and carefully thread 5 onto each of the soaked wooden skewers. Preheat the grill, then brush the grill rack with oil. Cook the skewers over hot coals or under a preheated hot broiler for 5–6 minutes, turning halfway through until cooked.

Serve the pork balls wrapped in lettuce leaves with the herbs and chili sauce.

This is the easiest and most delicious noodle dish in the world! Don't worry about deep-frying the noodles—they quickly puff up in a most satisfying fashion.

thai mee krob

Mix the dressing ingredients together in a small saucepan and cook, stirring, just until dissolved. Keep hot. Line 4 serving bowls with crumpled paper towels.

Heat the vegetable oil in a wok, add the curry paste, and cook for 1–2 minutes until the aromatics have been released. Add the pork strips and stir-fry until crisp, then add the shrimp, and stir-fry for about 1 minute until they turn opaque. Transfer to a dish and keep warm.

Wipe out the wok, fill one-third full of oil, and heat to 375°F or until a small piece of noodle fluffs up immediately.

Add a handful of noodles. Let puff and cook for 1 minute, then carefully turn over with tongs and cook the other side for 1 minute. Remove to one of the paper-lined bowls. Reheat the oil and repeat with the remaining noodles, reheating and skimming the oil as necessary. When all are ready, turn the noodles over in the bowls and discard the paper. Divide the pork, shrimp, and toppings between the bowls, drizzle over the dressing, and serve with chopsticks.

*Note Mild orange mussaman curry paste is sold in larger supermarkets and Thai shops. If unavailable, use another Thai curry paste, such as red or green.

1 tablespoon vegetable oil

1 tablespoon mussaman curry paste*

4 pork chops, boned and sliced

4–8 uncooked shrimp, peeled, tail fins intact, halved lengthwise

peanut oil, for frying

4 bundles dried wide ricestick noodles or fine rice vermicelli noodles

dressing

½ cup white rice vinegar

⅔ cup palm sugar or brown sugar

¼ cup soy sauce

¼ cup Thai fish sauce

toppings

8 scallions, sliced diagonally

6 baby Thai shallots, sliced (optional)

1 small package bean sprouts, trimmed

2 red chiles, seeded and sliced crosswise

sprigs of cilantro

serves 4

chicken dishes

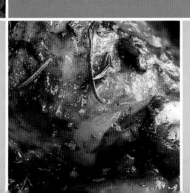

8 boneless chicken thighs or 4 breasts, skin on

3 teaspoons turmeric

3 whole star anise, crushed

3 garlic cloves, crushed

2 inches fresh ginger, finely sliced

grated zest of 1 lime and 1 tablespoon freshly squeezed lime juice

2 tablespoons Thai fish sauce

1 tablespoon dark soy sauce

2 tablespoons chili oil

1 tablespoon peanut oil

5 Chinese long beans, cut into 2 inch lengths (optional)

2 cups canned coconut milk

sliced red chiles, to serve

serves 4

This quick and easy Thai stir-fry makes a perfect midweek supper dish to share with friends.

thai marinated chicken stir-fried in chili oil

Place the chicken, skin side down, in a shallow non-metallic container. To marinate, rub in the turmeric, star anise, garlic, ginger, and lime zest, then sprinkle with the lime juice, fish sauce, soy sauce, and half the chili oil. Turn the chicken pieces in the mixture to coat well, cover, and leave in the refrigerator to marinate for 1 hour or overnight, turning at least once.

When ready to cook, drain, slice into ½ inch strips and reserve the marinade.

Heat a wok, add the peanut oil and remaining chili oil, then add the chicken pieces, skin side down. Cook at a high heat for 1–2 minutes until the skin is crispy, then turn down the heat and continue cooking until browned. Turn the pieces over and brown the other side.

Add the beans, reserved marinade, and the coconut milk. Stir well. Bring to a boil, stirring slowly; lower the heat and simmer for 10–15 minutes until the chicken is tender. Sprinkle with sliced red chile and serve with jasmine rice.

Chicken satay is one of the most popular Thai dishes. You can use it as part of a barbecue menu, whether Oriental or not, or as a party snack—the sticks make this very easy to nibble with drinks, and the peanut sauce is good as a dip with other foods, such as crudités.

chicken satay

To make the peanut sauce, heat the oil in a skillet until a light haze appears. Add the chopped garlic and sauté until golden brown. Add the curry paste, mix well, and cook for a few seconds. Add the coconut milk, mix well, and cook for a few seconds more. Add the stock, sugar, salt, and lemon juice and stir to blend. Cook for 1–2 minutes, constantly stirring. Add the ground peanuts, stir thoroughly, and pour the sauce into a bowl.

To make the satays, toast the coriander and cumin seeds gently in a small skillet without oil for about 5 minutes, stirring and shaking to make sure they don't burn. Remove from the heat and grind with a mortar and pestle to make a fine powder. (Use ready-ground spices if you are short of time.)

Using a sharp knife, cut the chicken breasts lengthwise into thin strips, about ⅛ inch wide. Put them in a bowl and add the ground toasted seeds, fish sauce, salt, peanut oil, curry powder, turmeric, coconut milk, and sugar. Mix thoroughly, cover with plastic wrap, and refrigerate for 8 hours or overnight (you can prepare them in the morning to serve in the evening).

Preheat a broiler or outdoor grill. Thread 2 pieces of the marinated chicken onto each skewer—not straight through the meat, but rather as if you were gathering or smocking a piece of fabric in a zigzag fashion. Grill or broil the satays until the meat is cooked through—6–8 minutes—turning to make sure they are browned on both sides. Serve with the peanut sauce and lemon or lime wedges.

2 teaspoons coriander seeds

2 teaspoons cumin seeds

4 skinless chicken breasts

2 tablespoons Thai fish sauce

1 teaspoon salt

¼ cup peanut or safflower oil

1 tablespoon curry powder

1 tablespoon ground turmeric

½ cup coconut milk

3 tablespoons sugar

lemon or lime wedges, to serve

peanut sauce

2 tablespoons peanut or safflower oil

3 garlic cloves, finely chopped

1 tablespoon panaeng curry paste or Thai red curry paste

½ cup coconut milk

1 cup chicken stock

1 tablespoon sugar

1 teaspoon salt

2 tablespoons freshly squeezed lemon or lime juice

¼ cup crushed roasted peanuts

8-inch wooden skewers, soaked in cold water for about 30 minutes

serves 4

4 chicken quarters (breasts or legs)

2 tablespoons peanut or safflower oil

1 teaspoon Chinese five-spice powder

1 inch fresh ginger, peeled and grated

½ teaspoon salt

3 tablespoons honey

1½ tablespoons dark soy sauce

ginger bok choy

3 tablespoons soy sauce

1 tablespoon sweet chili sauce

2 tablespoons peanut or safflower oil

2 teaspoons sesame oil

1 inch fresh ginger, peeled and finely sliced into matchstick strips

8 small bok choy, halved, well washed, and patted dry with paper towels

serves 4

Chinese five-spice powder is used widely in Asian cooking. It is made up of cassia bark (similar to cinnamon), cloves, fennel, star anise, and Szechuan pepper.

roast five-spice chicken with ginger bok choy

Preheat the oven to 400°F.

Wash and dry the chicken pieces and put in a roasting pan. Put the oil, five-spice powder, ginger, and salt in a bowl, mix well, then brush all over the chicken. Roast in the preheated oven for 25 minutes.

Put the honey and soy sauce in a small saucepan and heat until the honey has melted. Stir well, then brush all over the chicken to form a glaze. Return to the oven and roast for a further 10 minutes until the skin is crisp and golden.

To prepare the bok choy, put the soy sauce, chili sauce, and ¼ cup water in a bowl and mix well.

Heat the two oils in a wok or large skillet, add the ginger, and stir-fry for 30 seconds. Add the bok choy and continue to stir-fry for a further 2 minutes. Add the soy sauce mixture, cover, and simmer gently for 2 minutes, then serve with the chicken.

The authentic flavor of this curry comes from using fresh spices and the heady, slightly sour taste of bay leaves. Chicken thigh fillets work better here than breast meat as they are harder to overcook.

chicken and lentil curry with cucumber yogurt

Melt the butter in a deep skillet, add the onions, and fry, stirring, over medium heat. Once they are sizzling, cover with a lid, reduce the heat, and cook for 10–15 minutes, stirring occasionally.

When the onions have softened, add the garlic and garam masala, cook for a further 3–4 minutes until the spices start to release their aroma and the onions are beginning to turn golden. If you are using chicken thighs, add them now and cook for 5–6 minutes. Add the tomato juice, bay leaves, lentils, and stock. If you are using chicken breast, add it now. Cover with a lid and simmer for 15 minutes until the lentils are tender.

To make the cucumber yogurt, put the yogurt in a small dish, add a good pinch of salt, and stir in the cucumber.

When the curry is cooked, season generously with salt and freshly ground black pepper (lentils tend to absorb a lot of seasoning so don't be stingy). Transfer to bowls, scatter with cilantro, if using, and serve with a dollop of the cucumber yogurt to mix in. Serve with mango chutney and warm chapattis.

2 tablespoons butter or ghee (clarified butter)

2 large onions, thinly sliced

2 garlic cloves, peeled and crushed

1½ tablespoons garam masala (or ¼ teaspoon grated nutmeg; ½ teaspoon each ground cinnamon and ground pepper; 1 teaspoon ground cumin; and 10 cardamom pods, crushed)

1 lb. boneless chicken thigh or breast meat, cut into chunks

1¼ cups tomato juice

8 bay or curry leaves

⅔ cup red lentils

1¾ cups chicken stock

sea salt and freshly ground black pepper

cilantro leaves, to serve (optional)

cucumber yogurt

⅔ cup plain yogurt

¼ cucumber, cut into ribbons or chopped

serves 4

2 tablespoons rice wine, such as
Chinese Shaohsing or Japanese mirin

2 teaspoons cornstarch

12 oz. skinless chicken breasts

7 oz. Chinese dried egg noodles

3 tablespoons peanut or safflower oil

1 inch fresh ginger, peeled and
thinly sliced

4 oz. snow peas, finely sliced

1/4 cup chopped garlic chives or chives

4 oz. cashews, about 1 cup, toasted
in a dry skillet, then chopped

sauce

1/2 cup chicken stock

2 tablespoons dark soy sauce

1 tablespoon freshly squeezed
lemon juice

1 tablespoon toasted sesame oil

2 teaspoons light brown sugar

serves 4

*Most noodle dishes take just a matter of minutes to cook,
which makes them ideal for quick midweek suppers and
a welcome alternative to pasta.*

gingered chicken noodles

Put the rice wine and cornstarch in a bowl and mix well. Cut the chicken into
small chunks, add to the bowl, stir well, and set aside to marinate while you
prepare the remaining ingredients.

Soak the noodles according to the instructions on the package, then drain and
shake dry.

Put all the sauce ingredients in a small bowl and mix well.

Drain the chicken. Heat 1½ tablespoons of the oil in a wok or large skillet, then
add the chicken and stir-fry for 2 minutes until golden. Remove to a plate and
wipe the pan clean. Add the remaining 1½ tablespoons oil, ginger, and snow peas
and stir-fry for 1 minute. Return the chicken to the pan, then add the noodles
and sauce. Heat through for 2 minutes.

Add the garlic chives and cashews, stir well, and serve.

This is a dish from southeast India, where the people have a penchant for fiery food. It includes plenty of chiles combined with coriander seeds.

chettinad chicken

Using a mortar and pestle, blender, or spice mill, grind the dried chiles and toasted coriander seeds to a fine powder. Set aside.

To make the tarka, put the oil or ghee into a skillet and heat well. Add the turmeric, peppercorns, fennel and cumin seeds. Let sizzle briefly, then add the onion. Sauté for a few minutes, then add the ginger. Sauté for a further 6 minutes or so, until the onion is soft. If necessary, add a dash of water to prevent the mixture sticking to the pan.

Add the chicken and toss well to coat with the tarka. Sauté until the chicken begins to brown. Add enough water to cover, about 1⅓ cups, then the tomatoes. Bring to a boil, reduce the heat, and simmer gently until the chicken is cooked, about 8–10 minutes. A few minutes before the end of cooking time, stir in 1¼ tablespoons of the reserved ground chile-coriander spice blend (or more, to taste). Put the tamarind concentrate into a bowl, add a ladle of liquid, stir to dissolve, then stir into the pan. Sprinkle with the cilantro and top with the chiles, if using, then serve with yogurt.

8 large dried red chiles

2 tablespoons coriander seeds, toasted in a dry skillet

4 boneless, skinless chicken breasts, cut into chunks

3 tomatoes, chopped

2 teaspoons tamarind concentrate

sea salt

tarka spice-fry

2 tablespoons peanut oil or ghee (clarified butter)

¼ teaspoon turmeric

4 black peppercorns

¼ teaspoon fennel seeds

¼ teaspoon cumin seeds

1 medium onion, finely chopped

1 inch fresh ginger, peeled and grated

to serve

a handful of cilantro, chopped (optional)

2–4 green chiles, halved and seeded (optional)

plain yogurt

serves 4

This recipe is based on the classic Asian salt 'n' pepper squid. It makes a delicious chicken dish, guaranteed to become a family favorite at cookouts. Serve with a squeeze of fresh lime and chili sauce.

pepper 'n' spice chicken

To make the fragrant Asian rub, put the whole spices in a dry skillet and toast over medium heat for 1–2 minutes or until golden and aromatic. Remove from the heat and let cool. Transfer to a spice grinder and crush to a coarse powder. Alternatively, use a mortar and pestle. Put the spices into a bowl, add the garlic, lime zest, and salt and mix well. Set aside to infuse until ready to use.

Cut the chicken into 12 pieces and put in a dish. Add the rub and sesame oil and work well into the chicken pieces. Let marinate in the refrigerator for 2 hours, but return to room temperature for 1 hour before cooking.

Preheat the grill, then cook the chicken over medium hot coals for 15–20 minutes, turning after 10 minutes, until the chicken is cooked through and the juices run clear when the thickest part of the meat is pierced with a skewer. Squeeze with lime juice, let cool slightly, and serve with sweet chili sauce.

1 small chicken

2 tablespoons sesame oil

1–2 limes, cut into wedges

sweet chili sauce, to serve

fragrant asian rub

4 whole star anise

2 teaspoons Szechuan peppercorns

1 teaspoon fennel seeds

2 small pieces of cassia bark or 1 cinnamon stick, broken

6 cloves

2 garlic cloves, finely chopped

grated zest of 2 limes

1 teaspoon salt

an outdoor grill

serves 4

4 chicken legs (thigh and drumstick)

lemon or lime wedges, to serve

jerk seasoning paste

3–4 habanero chiles, seeded

1 teaspoon chopped thyme

3 garlic cloves, coarsely chopped

1 bay leaf

1 teaspoon allspice berries (about 20)

$^1/_4$ teaspoon freshly grated nutmeg

3 scallions, chopped

2 plum tomatoes, peeled (fresh or canned)

freshly squeezed juice of $^1/_2$ lime

$^1/_3$ cup peanut oil

$^1/_2$ teaspoon salt

serves 4

There are as many jerk chicken recipes in Jamaica as there are cooks, but all include the fiery Scotch bonnet chile or the closely related habanero, plus a good dose of native allspice. Traditionally grilled over wood, this recipe can easily be cooked in the oven or on an outdoor grill.

jerk chicken

To make the jerk seasoning paste put all the ingredients in a mortar and pestle or blender and grind to a smooth paste.

Cut slashes in the chicken legs and spread with half the jerk seasoning paste. Rub the paste all over and into the slashes, cover, and marinate in the refrigerator for at least 2 hours or overnight.

Preheat the oven to 400°F. Put the chicken legs skin side down into a roasting pan. Roast in the preheated oven for 40–45 minutes or until crisp and cooked through, turning halfway through the cooking time and coating with the remaining marinade.

Alternatively, preheat a charcoal grill until very hot. Cook the chicken over high heat to begin with, then adjust the rack further away from the fire as soon as the surfaces of the chicken have begun to brown. Cook for 15–20 minutes or until done, turning frequently and basting with the remaining marinade. You must cook poultry thoroughly so there is no pink inside: if you have an instant-read thermometer, it should read 165°F when inserted into the thickest part of the thigh.

Serve hot with lemon or lime wedges on the side for squeezing.

Chapattis are unleavened breads typically served as an accompaniment to spicy dishes in northern India, so they make the perfect wraps for this spicy Indian chicken topped with yogurt and cucumber relish.

indian chicken wraps
with minted cucumber relish

Preheat the oven to 400°F.

Cut the chicken fillets into strips. In a shallow dish, mix the curry paste, yogurt, and oil together. Add the chicken and toss to coat. Cover and leave to marinate for 30 minutes, or up to 4 hours, if time allows.

To make the relish, put the yogurt into a bowl with the cucumber, scallions, mint, and cumin. Mix together and season with black pepper. Chill.

Transfer the chicken pieces to a nonstick baking tray and bake for 15 minutes, or until the chicken juices run clear. Meanwhile, wrap the chapattis in foil and place in the oven to warm for the last 5 minutes, while the chicken is cooking.

Cut the chapattis in half. Top each half with a few strips of chicken and some spinach leaves, roll up, and secure with a toothpick. Serve 2 per person, along with a spoonful of the minted cucumber relish.

8 oz. skinless chicken breast fillets

2 tablespoons tandoori or tikka masala curry paste

3 tablespoons plain yogurt

2 teaspoons sunflower oil

4 chapattis

2 handfuls baby spinach leaves

minted cucumber relish

⅔ cup plain yogurt

¼ cucumber, seeded and diced

3 scallions, chopped

2 tablespoons chopped mint

½ teaspoon ground cumin

freshly ground black pepper

toothpicks

serves 4

3 tablespoons sunflower oil

16 oz. skinless chicken breast fillets, cut into strips

1 large onion, chopped

1 red chile, seeded and finely chopped

1 garlic clove, crushed

2 tablespoons tomato paste

14 oz. canned chopped tomatoes

14 oz. canned pinto beans, drained and rinsed

1 tablespoon chopped cilantro

8 corn tortillas, warmed

$^2/_3$ cup sour cream

2$^1/_2$ oz. sharp cheddar cheese, grated

salt and freshly ground black pepper

shredded scallions, to sprinkle

serves 4–6

Corn tortillas, pinto beans, and chiles are synonymous with Mexican cooking. This recipe combines chicken with a fiery tomato sauce as a filling for the soft tortillas, which are topped with sour cream and cheddar cheese before baking. It makes a perfect lunch or dinner dish served with a crisp leaf salad.

chili chicken enchiladas

Preheat the oven to 375°F.

Heat 2 tablespoons of the oil in a large nonstick skillet, add the chicken, and stir-fry for 4–5 minutes, or until golden. Remove with a slotted spoon, put into a bowl, and set aside.

Add the remaining oil to the pan, then the onion, and fry for 5 minutes. Add the chile and garlic and fry for 1–2 minutes more, or until the onions are soft and golden. Stir in the tomato paste, canned tomatoes, and $^1/_3$ cup cold water. Cook for 2–3 minutes and season with salt and freshly ground black pepper.

Add just under half the sauce to the chicken with the beans and cilantro and mix together. Spoon 2 heaped tablespoons of the chicken mixture onto the middle of each warmed tortilla and roll up to enclose the filling. Place seam-side down in a greased baking dish and top with the remaining tomato sauce.

Spoon the sour cream along the center of the tortillas and sprinkle with the grated cheese. Bake in the preheated oven for 15–20 minutes or until golden and bubbling. Sprinkle over the scallions and serve.

This Moroccan stew is both fruity and spicy, and the rosemary and ginger give it a delightful aroma. Serve it with couscous and a leafy green salad.

spicy chicken tagine
with apricots, rosemary, and ginger

Heat the oil and butter in a tagine or heavy-based casserole dish. Stir in the onion, chopped rosemary, ginger, and chiles and sauté until the onion begins to soften. Stir in the halved rosemary sprigs and the cinnamon sticks. Add the chicken thighs and brown them on both sides. Toss in the apricots with the honey, then stir in the plum tomatoes with their juice. (Add a little water if necessary, to ensure there is enough liquid to cover the base of the tagine and submerge the apricots.) Bring the liquid to a boil, then reduce the heat. Cover with a lid and cook gently for 35–40 minutes.

Season to taste with salt and pepper. Shred the larger basil leaves and leave the small ones intact. Sprinkle them over the chicken and serve the dish immediately.

2 tablespoons olive oil with a pat of butter

1 onion, finely chopped

3 sprigs of rosemary, 1 finely chopped, the other 2 cut in half

1½ inches fresh ginger, peeled and finely chopped

2 red chiles, seeded and finely chopped

1–2 cinnamon sticks

8 chicken thighs

¾ cup dried apricots

2 tablespoons clear honey

14 oz. canned plum tomatoes with their juice

sea salt and freshly ground black pepper

a small bunch of green or purple basil leaves

a tagine (optional)

serves 4

3 tablespoons vegetable oil

1 onion, roughly chopped

2 garlic cloves, crushed

1 tablespoon hot curry paste

1 tablespoon tomato paste

14 oz. canned chopped tomatoes
(flavored with mixed herbs, if available)

1 teaspoon red wine vinegar

2 broiled red bell peppers, chopped

1 zucchini, diced

1 lb. cooked chicken, cut into
bite-size pieces

sea salt and freshly ground
black pepper

cilantro sprigs, to garnish

serves 6

You can make this tantalizingly spicy chicken jalfrezi in less time than you might wait for a takeout. Use a jar of prepared broiled bell peppers and look out for good-quality curry pastes in supermarkets. Go for a hot variety containing spices such as chile, cumin, coriander, tamarind, and turmeric. Serve with jasmine rice and ready-cooked pappadoms.

chicken jalfrezi

Heat the oil in a large frying pan, reduce the heat, and add the onion and garlic. Sauté over medium heat until golden. Add the curry paste and cook for 1 minute to cook off the spices.

Add the tomato paste, chopped tomatoes, vinegar, and a scant cup water to the frying pan. Bring to a boil and simmer, uncovered, for 5 minutes.

Add the broiled bell peppers and diced zucchini and cook for a further 5 minutes until the zucchini are tender. Stir in the chicken pieces and season with salt and pepper. Simmer gently for another 6–7 minutes, or until the chicken is piping hot.

Add the cilantro at the last moment. Serve with jasmine rice and pappadoms.

You can add your choice of vegetables to this basic curry recipe, such as sliced mushrooms, trimmed green beans, fresh spinach, bamboo shoots, or sticks of zucchini and carrot—it's perfect for using up odds and ends. Jasmine or fragrant rice is a delicately scented white rice native to Thailand. If you are very short on time, use one of the excellent brands that is microwavable in the packet.

quick thai chicken curry

To make the jasmine rice, put the rice in a large pan that has a tight-fitting lid. Add 1½ cups cold water and the butter and salt. Bring to a boil, then turn down the heat to a simmer. Cook over low heat, covered, for 20 minutes, or until the rice has absorbed all the liquid (add a little more water if the rice is not tender).

Meanwhile, pour the coconut milk into a saucepan and gently bring it to near boiling. Remove the saucepan from the heat and stir in the Thai curry paste. Put to one side. Pour the oil into a large skillet or wok and stir-fry the chicken pieces over high heat until golden, about 2 minutes.

Pour the warm, spiced coconut milk over the fried chicken pieces and add the lime zest and fish sauce. Add any vegetables you are using at this stage. Stir and simmer gently for about 12 minutes, or until everything is cooked through.

Remove the cooked rice from the heat and let sit for 5 minutes. Fluff it up with a fork just before serving. Scatter the basil over the curry and serve it with a small bowl of the rice on the side.

1¾ cup canned coconut milk

3 tablespoons Thai green curry paste

1 tablespoon safflower oil

1 chicken breast (weighing about 14 oz.), cut into bite-sized pieces

1 teaspoon grated lime zest

1 teaspoon Thai fish sauce

4 oz. mixed fresh vegetables of your choice (see introduction)

a handful of basil leaves

jasmine rice

1 cup Thai jasmine or fragrant rice

2 tablespoons unsalted butter

a pinch of sea salt

serves 2

4 skinless and boneless chicken breasts, about 4½ oz. each

grated zest and freshly squeezed juice of 1 unwaxed lemon

1 tablespoon olive oil

1 teaspoon ground cumin

1 teaspoon paprika or smoked paprika

2 garlic cloves, crushed

2 tablespoons chopped parsley

2 tablespoons chopped cilantro

sea salt and freshly ground black pepper

tomato pilaf

1 large eggplant, cut into ½ inch dice

4 ripe tomatoes, chopped

1 teaspoon cumin seeds

2 garlic cloves, crushed

2 teaspoons tomato paste

¾ cup basmati rice

14 oz. canned chickpeas, drained and rinsed

1 cup boiling water

1 teaspoon olive oil

serves 4

Chermoula is a fragrant North African paste that is often used as a marinade for fish, but works just as well with chicken. Instead of tomato pilaf, you could serve this with plain rice if you are short of time.

chermoula chicken with tomato pilaf

Toss the diced eggplant for the pilaf with a pinch of salt and set aside in a colander for 15 minutes to draw out the excess liquid.

Lightly slash the chicken breasts so that the marinade will be able to permeate the meat. Mix the lemon zest and juice with the olive oil, cumin, paprika, garlic, parsley, cilantro, and seasoning. Rub into the chicken, cover, and set aside in a baking dish in a cool place while cooking the pilaf.

To make the pilaf, put the tomatoes, cumin seeds, garlic, tomato paste, and 2 tablespoons water in a large saucepan and simmer rapidly for 5–6 minutes until thick and quite dry. Stir in the rice, chickpeas, boiling water, and a pinch of salt. Bring back to a boil, stir the rice once, then cover the pan tightly and leave to simmer on the lowest heat for 20 minutes.

Preheat the oven to 400°F. As soon as the rice is cooking, squeeze the liquid from the eggplant and pat dry on paper towels. Toss with the olive oil and spread out on a baking sheet. Put on the highest shelf in the preheated oven, with the dish of chicken on the shelf below. Cook for 15–18 minutes, stirring the eggplant halfway through cooking to brown evenly.

Stir the roasted eggplant into the tomato pilaf, then serve the chermoula chicken breasts on top. Serve with a green vegetable.

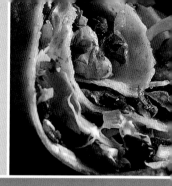

vegetarian dishes

1 tablespoon olive oil

1 onion, thinly chopped

1 garlic clove, crushed

1 tablespoon harissa paste

14 oz. canned chickpeas, drained

14 oz. canned chopped tomatoes
(flavored with garlic or mixed herbs,
if available)

4 oz. halloumi cheese, cut into cubes

3½ oz. baby spinach leaves

sea salt and freshly ground
black pepper

freshly squeezed juice of ½ lemon

freshly grated Parmesan cheese, to serve

serves 2

Halloumi is a firm Cypriot cheese that is delicious eaten when hot and melting. It has a reasonably long shelf-life before it is opened, which means you can keep a pack tucked away in the fridge. Harissa is a fiery chili paste used in North African cooking—add more than the tablespoon here if you like your food very spicy.

harissa-spiced chickpeas *with halloumi and spinach*

Pour the oil into a large pan and gently sauté the onion and garlic until softened. Add the harissa paste, chickpeas, and chopped tomatoes. Bring to a boil and let simmer for about 5 minutes.

Add the halloumi cheese and spinach, cover, and cook over a low heat for a further 5 minutes. Season to taste and stir in the lemon juice. Spoon onto serving plates and sprinkle with the Parmesan cheese. Serve immediately with a crisp green side salad.

*This tasty dish makes a delicious TV dinner or can be
served as a midweek supper for friends and family.*

vegetable burritos

Preheat the oven to 400°F.

To make the salsa, mix all the ingredients together. Cover
and chill until ready to use.

Put the tomatoes in a saucepan with the garlic, chili
powder, oregano, and tomato paste. Bring to a boil, reduce
the heat, and simmer for 10 minutes, until the mixture
reduces slightly and begins to thicken.

Meanwhile, heat the oil in a separate saucepan. Add the
peppers and sauté for 5 minutes, until soft. Add the peppers
to the tomato mixture. Put the refried beans in a saucepan
and heat gently, stirring frequently until piping hot.

Wrap the tortillas in foil and warm in the preheated oven
for 6–7 minutes, until soft and piping hot, or heat
according to the instructions on the packet. Remove from
the oven and put the tortillas on 4 serving plates. Spread
each tortilla with a thick layer of beans, then 1 tablespoon
of the tomato and pepper mixture, a quarter of the cheese,
1 tablespoon of salsa, and ½ tablespoon of sour cream.
Sprinkle with cilantro, fold, and serve immediately.

14 oz. canned chopped tomatoes

3 garlic cloves, crushed

1 tablespoon mild chili powder,
or to taste

a pinch of dried oregano

1 tablespoon tomato paste

1 tablespoon olive oil

1 yellow bell pepper, seeded and sliced

1 green bell pepper, seeded and sliced

14 oz. canned refried beans, or canned
borlotti or pinto beans, drained, rinsed,
and mashed

4 large wheat tortillas

3½ oz. extra-sharp cheddar
cheese, grated

2 tablespoons reduced-fat sour cream

2 tablespoons chopped cilantro

sea salt and freshly ground black pepper

salsa

½ large red onion, chopped

2 tomatoes, chopped

½ green chile, seeded and finely chopped

1 tablespoon freshly squeezed lime juice

1 tablespoon chopped mint

serves 4

If you are looking for a tasty and filling meal, try this recipe. Sweet potatoes make a nutritious alternative to ordinary potatoes and as they stay moist during cooking, there is no need to add extra butter.

baked sweet potato
with mexican beans

4 sweet potatoes, about 6½ oz. each

1 tablespoon olive oil

1 onion, finely chopped

2 garlic cloves, crushed (optional)

2 red chiles, seeded and finely chopped

2 tablespoons red wine vinegar

1 tablespoon Worcestershire sauce

20 oz. canned chopped tomatoes

14 oz. canned mixed beans, drained and rinsed

1 tablespoon chopped cilantro

2 oz. extra-sharp cheddar cheese, grated, to serve (optional)

serves 4

Preheat the oven to 400°F.

Scrub the potatoes and prick all over with a fork. Cook the potatoes in the preheated oven for 1–1¼ hours, or until soft. Alternatively, wrap the potatoes in parchment paper and microwave each one on high for 3½–4 minutes, or until soft. Let the potatoes stand for 1 minute.

Heat the oil in a nonstick saucepan. Add the onion, garlic, chiles, red wine vinegar, and Worcestershire sauce. Sauté until the onions are soft, about 5 minutes. Add the tomatoes to the pan, bring to a boil, lower the heat, and simmer for 10 minutes. Add the beans, stir, and cook for a few minutes more, until they are piping hot. Stir in the cilantro.

Cut the sweet potatoes in half. Put 2 halves on each serving plate and spoon the Mexican beans over the top. Sprinkle with some grated cheddar cheese, if using, and serve immediately.

½ cup polenta grain

½ cup plain flour

3 eggs

about 1 cup low-fat milk

2 garlic cloves

2 red onions

12 patty pan squash

2 red bell peppers

1 pickled red jalapeño chile

1 tablespoon olive oil, plus extra for frying

2 tablespoons cilantro, chopped

salt

tomato salsa

4 ripe tomatoes

2 scallions

1 red chile

2 tablespoons red wine vinegar

serves 4

These pretty yellow pancakes, made with polenta, have a sweet, nutty texture. Add a dollop of sour cream and this dish could be served by itself for lunch, or as an appetizer.

corn crêpes
with chili vegetables and tomato salsa

To make the crêpes, place the polenta grain, plain flour, and salt in a bowl, then beat in the eggs and milk to form a smooth batter. Set aside.

To make the filling, crush the garlic, slice the onions, and cut the squash in quarters. Seed and chop the red bell peppers and pickled chile. Heat 1 tablespoon oil in a skillet, add the garlic, onions, squash, bell peppers, chile, and a pinch of salt, and sauté gently until just tender.

To make the salsa, roughly chop the tomatoes and finely chop the scallions. Seed and roughly chop the red chile, then mix all the ingredients together and chill until ready to use.

To cook the crêpes, heat the oil in a 7 inch skillet. Add a ladle of crêpe batter and swirl around so the mixture covers the base. Cook until the surface bubbles and the base is browned, then turn and brown the other side. Remove and set aside in a warm place while you cook the remaining crêpes.

Spoon the filling into the crêpes, top with cilantro, and serve immediately with the tomato salsa.

This mixture of squash, plantains, bell peppers, and peas simmered in a chile and coconut stock is delicious served with basmati rice.

caribbean curry

To prepare the butternut squash, cut in half, remove and discard the seeds, peel off the skin and cut the flesh into chunky cubes. Heat the chili oil in a large saucepan, add the sliced chiles, cinnamon sticks, and cloves and let them sizzle to release their aromas. Stir in the onions and cook until softened and a little golden. Stir in the squash and plantain, add the vegetable stock and coconut milk, bring to a boil, and simmer for 10 minutes.

Add the lemon juice, bell pepper, and peas, cook for a further 10 minutes, and serve. Basmati rice would be a suitable accompaniment.

2 butternut squash

1 tablespoon chili oil

2 red chiles, seeded and sliced

2 cinnamon sticks

6 cloves

1 onion, roughly chopped

1 plantain, peeled and thickly sliced

1¼ cups vegetable stock

⅔ cup canned coconut milk

1 teaspoon freshly squeezed lemon juice

1 green bell pepper, seeded and cut into chunks

1 cup fresh or frozen peas

serves 4

Although it may sound unusual, chocolate is the secret ingredient of this Mexican-inspired dish. It adds a wonderfully rich, intense flavor to the vegetables. Serve with boiled rice or cornbread.

quick vegetarian mole

Heat the oil in a saucepan and sauté the onion, pepper, garlic, and spices for 5 minutes. Add the sweet potatoes, tomatoes, beans, chili sauce, and 1¼ cups water and bring to a boil. Cover and simmer over gentle heat for 30 minutes.

Stir in the chocolate and cilantro and cook for a final 5 minutes. Taste and adjust the seasoning with salt and pepper, then serve with rice or cornbread.

2 tablespoons peanut or safflower oil

1 red onion, chopped

1 large red bell pepper, seeded and chopped

2 garlic cloves

2 teaspoons ground coriander

1 teaspoon ground cumin

½ teaspoon ground cinnamon

1 lb. sweet potatoes, cut into cubes

1 lb. canned chopped tomatoes, about 2 cups

1 lb. canned red kidney beans, rinsed and drained, about 2 cups

1–2 teaspoons sweet chili sauce

1 oz. dark chocolate, grated

2 tablespoons chopped cilantro

sea salt and freshly ground black pepper

serves 4

The potato, known as aloo in several Indian languages, is an important ingredient for the large vegetarian Hindu population. It has revolutionized nutrition in high mountain areas, where the potato yield is more reliable than the grain crops it replaced.

2 large eggplants

1½ lb. waxy potatoes, peeled and cut into ½ inch cubes

6–8 tablespoons vegetable oil

1 tablespoon cumin seeds

1 teaspoon black mustard seeds

1 teaspoon sesame seeds

1 onion, finely chopped

1–2 garlic cloves, crushed

1 teaspoon grated fresh ginger

1 green chile, seeded and finely chopped

½ teaspoon ground turmeric

1 teaspoon ground coriander

½ teaspoon salt, plus extra for sprinkling

1–2 tablespoons freshly squeezed lemon or lime juice

to serve

4 tablespoons plain yogurt

garam masala, for sprinkling

2 tablespoons chopped cilantro

serves 4

indian dry potato curry
in eggplant shells

Cut the eggplants in half lengthwise and, using a spoon, scoop out the flesh, leaving a ¼ inch shell. Cut the flesh into ½ inch dice. Sprinkle the inside of the eggplant shells with salt and put in a colander, cut side down. Spread the eggplant cubes on a plate or tray or in a colander and sprinkle with more salt. Leave for about 30 minutes, then rinse well and pat dry with paper towels.

Preheat the oven to 375°F. Bring a saucepan of lightly salted water to a boil, add the potato cubes, and cook for 5 minutes. Drain well and let cool. Place the eggplant shells, cut side up, on a baking tray, brush with 2 tablespoons of the oil, and bake in the preheated oven for 10 to 15 minutes until softened. Remove from the oven and turn the eggplant shells upside down on a plate to drain off any excess oil.

Heat another 2 tablespoons of the oil in a large skillet, add the cumin, mustard, and sesame seeds and when they start to pop add the onion, garlic, ginger, and chile. Stir-fry for about 2 to 3 minutes then add the eggplant cubes. Cook, stirring occasionally, for 4–5 minutes or until they are just cooked, adding more oil as needed.

Stir in the turmeric, ground coriander, and salt, then add the potatoes and stir-fry for 5–6 minutes until the potatoes are golden. Remove from the heat and stir in the lemon or lime juice. Taste and adjust the seasoning.

Put the eggplants back on the baking tray, cut side up. Divide the potato mixture evenly between them and return to the oven for 10 minutes to heat through. Serve with the yogurt and sprinkle with a little garam masala and the chopped cilantro.

1¼ cups yellow lentils

3 tablespoons oil

½ teaspoon mustard seeds

½ teaspoon fenugreek seeds

1 teaspoon grated fresh ginger

1 teaspoon crushed garlic

1 teaspoon cayenne pepper

1½ teaspoons ground coriander

½ teaspoon ground turmeric

4 tomatoes, skinned and chopped

1 teaspoon salt

1½ lb. floury potatoes, peeled and diced

to serve

2 tablespoons chopped cilantro, plus extra sprigs, to garnish

½ teaspoon garam masala

serves 4

Rice and lentils is a staple meal for millions of Indians and Nepalis. In this recipe, potatoes are added to that traditional duo. They are particularly desirable for their ability to absorb the wonderful flavors of Indian spices.

indian potato curry with yellow lentils

Wash the lentils well in several changes of water.

Heat the oil in a large saucepan over a low heat. Add the mustard and fenugreek seeds. When they begin to pop, stir in the ginger and garlic and sauté for 30 seconds.

Add the cayenne pepper, ground coriander, and turmeric and stir-fry for a further 30 seconds. Add the tomatoes and lentils to the pan, cover with 2¾ cups water, add the salt, and bring to a boil. Reduce the heat, cover, and simmer for 20–30 minutes or until the lentils are just soft. Add the potatoes and simmer over a low heat for 10–15 minutes or until tender. Taste and adjust the seasoning.

Sprinkle with chopped cilantro and garam masala, add sprigs of cilantro, and serve with basmati rice, naan bread, or both.

We have Mexico to thank for the introduction of chiles to the rest of the world. This recipe calls for smoky chipotle chile, as well as cumin seeds.

burritos with black beans
and avocado salsa

Put 2 of the garlic cloves and the beans into a saucepan, add enough water to cover the beans by 1 inch, bring to a boil, reduce the heat, cover, and cook for 1½–2 hours or until the beans are very tender (cooking time depends on the age of the beans). Drain the beans, reserving the cooking liquid.

Crush the remaining garlic and chop the chiles. Heat the oil in a large saucepan and add the chiles and cumin. Sauté for 20 seconds, then add the onion. Sauté for about 5 minutes, then add the crushed garlic. Cook for a further 3–4 minutes or until the onion is soft. Add the drained beans, together with a little of their cooking liquid to keep them moist. Continue to cook, stirring frequently. Season with salt and pepper and mash well, adding enough liquid to make a chunky paste. Cover.

To make the salsa, scoop out the avocado flesh and cut into smallish chunks. Put it into a bowl with the lime juice, tossing well so the avocado doesn't discolor. Add the red onion and cherry tomatoes, then stir in the sugar and cilantro. Mix well, cover, and set aside.

Wrap the tortillas in foil and warm in a medium oven for 6–7 minutes, until piping hot, or heat according to the instructions on the package. Gently reheat the beans, add the scallions and cilantro, and stir gently. Put a small portion of beans onto each tortilla and carefully roll into a burrito. Put a little salsa onto each plate. Let guests help themselves to lettuce and crème fraîche or yogurt.

3 garlic cloves

1 cup dried black beans, soaked overnight and drained

2 chipotle chiles

2 tablespoons corn or olive oil

1½ teaspoons cumin seeds

1 onion, finely chopped

6 flour tortillas

2–4 scallions, chopped

a handful of cilantro, chopped

sea salt and freshly ground black pepper

avocado salsa

1 avocado

freshly squeezed juice of 1 lime

1 large red onion, chopped

10 cherry tomatoes, quartered

½ teaspoon sugar

¼ cup chopped cilantro

to serve

a handful of shredded lettuce

crème fraîche or plain yogurt

**serves 6 as an appetizer
or 3 as an entrée**

Szechuan peppercorns are an important spice in Chinese cookery, included in the well-known blend of Chinese five-spice. Not related to black pepper, Szechuan peppercorns are unusual in appearance and taste. They are used in a simple stir-fry here, where their effect can best be appreciated. They are readily available in Chinese stores. Serve this dish with noodles or rice.

vegetable stir-fry
with szechuan peppercorns

Discard any shiny black inner seeds from the peppercorns. Toast the peppercorns in a small skillet over low heat for 1–2 minutes until aromatic. Using a mortar and pestle, grind to a coarse powder.

Heat the peanut oil in a wok and add the scallions and garlic. Stir-fry over medium-high heat for 1 minute. Add the pepper, carrot, baby corn, lemon juice, and 1 tablespoon of the soy sauce and stir-fry for 2–3 minutes.

Add the broccoli, sugar snap peas, ground Szechuan pepper, and the remaining soy sauce. Stir-fry briefly, cover, and cook for 4–5 minutes or until the vegetables are tender but still firm. Uncover and add the sesame oil. Stir and serve hot with a small dish of ground Szechuan pepper for guests to help themselves.

1 teaspoon Szechuan peppercorns, plus extra to serve

2 tablespoons peanut oil

4 scallions, chopped

2 garlic cloves, sliced

1 small red bell pepper, seeded and finely sliced lengthwise

1 carrot, finely sliced lengthwise into matchstick strips

18 baby corn (candle corn), chopped into 3

freshly squeezed juice of ½ lemon

¼ cup dark soy sauce

1 small head of broccoli, broken into florets

14 sugar snap peas, trimmed

1 tablespoon sesame oil

serves 4

This Provençal-style tian is cooked in a wide, shallow, open casserole dish. The chorizo adds an extra dimension for non-vegetarians but is optional.

capsicum chili tian
with goat cheese

4 red bell peppers

2 yellow or orange bell peppers

½ cup extra virgin olive oil, plus extra for brushing and drizzling

2 small mild chorizo sausages, finely sliced (optional)

a handful of basil leaves, plus extra for scattering

12 cherry tomatoes, halved

2 red onions, finely chopped

1–2 medium-hot red chiles, seeded and finely sliced

about 8 oz. mature goat cheese, cut into 12 chunks

lemon wedges, to serve

salt, preferably sea salt flakes, and freshly ground black pepper

pesto

a large bunch of basil

a large handful of parsley leaves

¼ cup olive oil

¼ cup pine nuts

2 garlic cloves, crushed

1 cup grated Parmesan cheese

serves 4

To make the pesto, put the basil, parsley, olive oil, pine nuts, and garlic in a blender and process until smooth. Add the Parmesan, then blend again. Preheat the oven to 400°F.

Cut the bell peppers in half lengthwise through the stalk. Carefully remove the cores. Put the bell peppers in a plastic bag, add the ½ cup olive oil, salt, and pepper, then shake until well coated with oil.

Brush a shallow tian or casserole dish with extra olive oil and add the peppers, cut side up, cramming them close together. Put a slice of chorizo (if using), a basil leaf, a halved cherry tomato, a spoonful of pesto, some onion, a little chile, and a chunk of goat cheese in each pepper half. Drizzle more oil over the top.

Cook in the preheated oven for about 30 minutes, or until the peppers are tender and crispy brown at the edges and the cheese is melted and bubbling.

Serve on small plates with extra basil leaves scattered over the top, wedges of lemon for squeezing, and a salad. Char-grilled Italian bread is perfect for mopping up the delicious juices.

Curry originated in the Indian subcontinent and migrated eastwards toward Thailand long before it traveled west to Europe and North America. Thai curries are generally even hotter and more flavorful than their Indian cousins. Choose a brand of red curry paste that is made in Thailand if you can.

vegetable curry

Put the oil in a saucepan, heat well, then quickly stir in the curry paste. Add the coconut cream, mixing well. Add the vegetable stock and stir briefly.

Add the long beans, carrots, corn, cauliflower, lime leaves, chiles, soy sauce, sugar, salt, and eggplant. Stir well, then cook for a few minutes until the vegetables are tender.

Add the basil leaves, stir once, then ladle into a bowl and serve with jasmine rice.

2 tablespoons peanut or safflower oil

2 tablespoons Thai red curry paste

2¾ cups coconut cream

2¾ cups vegetable stock

4 Chinese long beans, cut into 1 inch pieces

4 carrots, cut into matchsticks

5 ears of baby corn, cut into 1 inch pieces

½ cup cauliflower, cut into florets

4 kaffir lime leaves, coarsely chopped

2 large red or green chiles, coarsely sliced

3 tablespoons light soy sauce

2 teaspoons sugar

½ teaspoon salt

6 small round green eggplant, quartered

30 basil leaves

serves 4

sunflower oil, for greasing

large flour tortillas

cheddar cheese, grated, feta cheese,
crumbled, or cream cheese

fillings

chopped tomatoes

chopped scallions

chopped red chiles

sliced pickled jalapeño chiles

finely sliced zucchini

sliced mushrooms

chopped bell peppers

chopped avocado

pitted black olives

mashed, canned beans such as refried,
black, pinto, or borlotti beans

ground cumin

pimentón (Spanish oak-smoked paprika)

to serve (optional)

chopped cilantro

plain yogurt, crème fraîche,
or sour cream

serve 1 tortilla per person

Quantities for these excellent snacks are not given here as there's no need, just pile on as much filling as you like. Fried, grilled or baked, this Mexican snack also makes excellent party food.

quesadillas

Lightly grease a large skillet with 1 teaspoon of oil. Lay a tortilla flat in the pan and cover with cheese and 4 or 5 fillings of your choice. Top with a second tortilla and press down gently. Cook over a moderate heat until the bottom tortilla is golden and crisp, about 5–7 minutes. Cover with a plate, turn the pan over, and lift it off. Slide the inverted quesadilla back into the pan and cook as before. Cut into triangles.

Serve with chopped cilantro and yogurt, crème fraîche, or sour cream, if using.

Variation To broil or bake the quesadillas, put a tortilla on a lightly greased baking sheet, top with cheese, preferably cheddar, and add 4–5 fillings of your choice. Cook under a hot broiler or in a preheated oven at 350°F for 10 minutes or until the cheese is golden.

Based on a charred, then puréed eggplant, this unusual curry is incredibly good. It can be made in advance and, in fact, improves by being left overnight so that all the spicy flavors can develop.

charred eggplant and coconut curry

To make the spice paste, dry-toast the spice seeds in a skillet, shaking until they pop and turn lightly golden. Transfer to a blender or spice grinder, add the remaining ingredients and ⅓ cup water, and grind to a smooth paste. Set aside.

Roast the eggplant directly over a high gas flame until charred and softened, about 15 minutes. Alternatively, roast in a preheated oven at 425°F for about 40 minutes. Let cool, then peel and discard the skin. Don't worry if a few charred bits remain—this will add extra flavor.

Heat the oil or ghee in a large, heavy-based saucepan, add the onion, and cook until softened. Add the spice paste and stir for 2 minutes to release the aromas, then add the pepper, sweet potatoes, zucchini, and chickpeas. Cover and cook, stirring occasionally, for 10 minutes. Add the tomatoes and 1 cup water, then bring to a boil and simmer, uncovered, for about 20 minutes.

Put the peeled eggplant in a blender, add the coconut milk, and pulse to a coarse purée. Add to the pan and bring back to a simmer. Add salt, if necessary. Cook for 10 minutes, then remove from the heat, cover, and let stand for at least 30 minutes or preferably overnight.

Reheat, then top with cilantro sprigs and serve with rice, yogurt, and mango chutney.

1 medium eggplant, about 8 oz.

2 tablespoons vegetable oil or ghee (clarified butter)

1 red onion, chopped

1 red bell pepper, chopped

1½ cups peeled and diced sweet potatoes, about 8 oz.

1 medium zucchini, about 8 oz.

16 oz. canned chickpeas, drained and rinsed

16 oz. canned chopped tomatoes

1 cup unsweetened canned coconut milk

sprigs of cilantro, to serve

kosher salt or sea salt, to taste

spice paste

1 tablespoon cumin seeds

1 tablespoon coriander seeds

seeds from 10 cardamom pods

½ teaspoon fenugreek seeds

2 inches fresh ginger, peeled and grated

4 garlic cloves

1 teaspoon ground turmeric

1–2 serrano chiles, seeded, or 1 teaspoon hot pepper flakes

1 tomato, quartered

2 teaspoons kosher salt or sea salt

1 teaspoon sugar

serves 4–6

1 lb. halloumi cheese, sliced

2 red onions, halved and cut into wedges

1 red bell pepper, seeded and
cut into strips

1 yellow bell pepper, seeded and
cut into strips

1 green bell pepper, seeded and
cut into strips

1 medium or 2 small zucchini, quartered
lengthwise and cut into chunks

8 oz. button mushrooms

8–10 large flour tortillas

marinade

2 garlic cloves

1 tablespoon coarse kosher salt
or sea salt

grated zest of 2 limes

freshly squeezed juice of 4 limes

a handful of cilantro, chopped

½ teaspoon dried oregano

½ teaspoon hot red pepper flakes

1 teaspoon cumin seeds

1 teaspoon sugar

1 tablespoon white wine vinegar

½ cup dark rum

½ cup olive oil

to serve

ready-made guacamole

tomato salsa (page 201)

sour cream, crème fraîche, or plain yogurt

serves 4–6

Fajitas—usually made with beef or chicken—are utterly delicious and can be adapted easily for vegetarians, using halloumi. This firm cheese from Cyprus is unique; it won't melt when fried and develops a delicious crisp crust. Eat the fajitas as soon as you make them; the halloumi loses tenderness if left for too long after cooking.

halloumi fajitas

To make the marinade, crush the garlic and salt to a paste in a mortar and pestle. Transfer to a bowl, add the remaining ingredients, except the oil, and whisk together. Add the oil in a steady stream, whisking until the mixture has emulsified. Put the halloumi in a shallow dish, add enough marinade to cover, and turn until coated. Put the onions, peppers, zucchini, and mushrooms in a bowl, add the remaining marinade, and mix well. Cover both dishes and let marinate in the refrigerator for at least 30 minutes.

Preheat the oven to 300°F. Stack the tortillas, wrap in foil, and put in the preheated oven for about 15 minutes until warm. Meanwhile, heat a large skillet or wok until very hot, add the marinated vegetables and liquid, and stir-fry until the juices have evaporated and the vegetables are golden and slightly caramelized, about 20 minutes. Transfer to a heatproof dish, cover, and keep warm in the oven. Drain the halloumi, discarding the marinade. Put the slices in the skillet or wok in a single layer. Cook over a moderate heat for about 10 minutes, turning halfway through cooking, until golden.

Serve the tortillas, vegetables, and cheese separately, so that people can make their own fajitas. To assemble, put a warm tortilla on a plate, add a spoonful of vegetables to one half and top with halloumi. Bring the uncovered half of the tortilla up over the filling, then tuck the corners underneath the fajitas. Serve with guacamole, salsa, and lots of sour cream, crème fraîche, or yogurt.

¾ cup jasmine or long-grain
rice, washed

⅔ cup vegetable stock

⅔ cup peanut oil

4 large eggs

2 garlic cloves, peeled and crushed

4 scallions, sliced

1 teaspoon sesame oil

1 tablespoon light soy sauce

a good pinch of white pepper

2 tablespoons oyster sauce

2 red chiles, seeded and finely chopped

a handful of cilantro leaves

serves 2

A dish from a restaurant in Sydney was the inspiration for this recipe. To eat, tear up the egg with chopsticks and mix the frazzled whites and molten yolks into the rice.

deep-fried eggs
with rice, chile, and oyster sauce

Put the rice and stock in a small saucepan, cover, and cook over high heat. Once it is boiling, reduce the heat as low as it will go and let bubble away gently for 8–10 minutes, or until the rice has swelled and absorbed all the water. Turn off the heat and let it steam on its own for another 10 minutes.

Pour the peanut oil into a wok or large saucepan and heat until hot—throw in a cube of bread and if it browns in 10 seconds, the oil is hot enough. Crack 2 of the eggs into a dish, then gently slide them into the wok. It will hiss and splutter, so stand back for a couple of seconds. Cook for 1–2 minutes until the whites are set but the yolks still oozy, then transfer with a slotted spoon onto a plate. Cook the remaining eggs in the same way.

Pour away all but 1 tablespoon of the peanut oil (you can bottle it and use it again once cool) and add the garlic. Cook until it is starting to color, then tip in the cooked rice and half the scallions. Stir-fry briskly, then add the sesame oil, soy sauce, and white pepper. Give it a good stir, then transfer to 2 bowls. Put a portion of egg on each mound of rice, drizzle with oyster sauce, and sprinkle over the chiles, remaining scallions, and the cilantro leaves.

Pulses such as split peas and lentils are a good source of protein for vegetarians and they work well as a base for hot chiles. In India, dhal is a traditional accompaniment to rice, flatbreads, and curried vegetables or meats.

12 oz. yellow split peas, washed

½ teaspoon ground turmeric

1 teaspoon salt

3 tablespoons vegetable oil

1 teaspoon cumin seeds

1 cinnamon stick

3–5 dried, hot red chiles

8 oz. spinach leaves

2 tablespoons shredded coconut, or coconut flakes, toasted (optional)

serves 4

spinach dhal
with toasted coconut

Place the split peas in a saucepan, add the turmeric, and about 4 cups water. Bring to a boil, then cover with the lid slightly ajar. Reduce the heat and simmer for about 20 minutes, then add salt and cook for about 15–20 minutes more, until the split peas are cooked and tender, and have absorbed all the liquid.

Heat the oil in a small skillet until very hot, add the cumin seeds, cinnamon, and chiles, and gently sauté to release the aromas. Add the spinach and sauté for a few minutes until the leaves turn bright green.

Pile the spiced spinach on heated plates and spoon the yellow dhal beside. Sprinkle with shredded or toasted coconut, if using, and serve.

Red lentils are widely used in Indian cooking to make dhal. They are healthy, nutritious, and delicious. Serve this dish as part of an Indian meal.

curried red lentils

Put the onion, garlic, and ginger in a food processor and blend to form a fairly smooth purée. Heat the butter in a saucepan, add the purée, tomatoes, and spices, and sauté gently for about 5 minutes.

Add the lentils, stock, lemon juice, salt, and pepper, bring to a boil, cover, and simmer over low heat for about 20 minutes until the lentils have thickened.

Taste and adjust the seasoning with salt and pepper, then serve topped with a few fried curry leaves, if using.

1 onion, chopped

2 garlic cloves, chopped

1 inch fresh ginger, peeled and grated

4 tablespoons unsalted butter

12 oz. tomatoes, chopped

1 tablespoon curry powder

1 teaspoon ground turmeric

½ teaspoon ground cinnamon

12 oz. red lentils, about 1¾ cups

4 cups vegetable stock

freshly squeezed juice of ½ lemon

sea salt and freshly ground black pepper

2–3 sprigs of fresh or frozen curry leaves, fried for a few seconds in 2 tablespoons unsalted butter (optional)

serves 6

Baath masala is a South Indian spice mixture. Make a batch and use it for other spiced rice dishes, adding green bell peppers instead of the dill, or a mixture of vegetables like carrots, peas, and green beans.

south indian spiced rice

To make the baath masala, put the yellow lentils into a skillet and dry-roast over medium heat for 30 seconds or so, stirring all the time. Add the white lentils, chiles, cloves, cardamom pod, cinnamon sticks, coconut, and coriander seeds. Dry-roast, stirring constantly, until you can smell a toasted aroma and steam begins rising from the pan. Transfer to a mortar and pestle or spice-grinder. Grind coarsely and set aside until ready to use.

Put the rice into a wide, heavy saucepan with a tight-fitting lid. Add 3¾ cups water and bring to a boil. Reduce the heat to the lowest setting. Line the inside of the lid with a dish towel and cover tightly so that no steam escapes. (This step is very important—gather the edges of the towel and fold over the top of the lid to keep the towel from coming into contact with the flame.) Gently simmer for 15 minutes, then turn off the heat completely and let steam, still tightly covered, for a further 10 minutes. For perfect results, do not uncover the rice at any time.

Put the 3 tablespoons oil or ghee into a small saucepan and heat until hot. Add the mustard seeds, yellow and white lentils, cumin seeds, and turmeric all at once. Cover the pan, reduce the heat to medium, and let the spices sizzle and pop. Remove the pan from the heat and add the chopped dill, 3 tablespoons of the baath masala, and salt. Stir over low heat until the dill is nicely wilted and the masala is well mixed—add a little water if necessary. Remove from the heat.

Transfer the cooked rice to a large mixing bowl, fluff up with a fork, and sprinkle ⅓ cup oil over the top. Add the dill mixture and ¼ cup more baath masala and mix well so the rice is coated—use two forks or your hands to make sure the herbs and masala coat all the rice. Serve warm.

1¾ cups basmati rice

3 tablespoons safflower oil or ghee (clarified butter)

1 tablespoon black mustard seeds

1 teaspoon yellow lentils

1 teaspoon white lentils

1 teaspoon cumin seeds

½ teaspoon ground turmeric

4 oz. dill, central and any tough stems discarded, fronds chopped

⅓ cup safflower oil

sea salt

baath masala (spice mix)

¼ cup yellow lentils

¼ cup white lentils

7 medium dried red chiles

9 whole cloves

1 cardamom pod

2 cinnamon sticks, broken into pieces

¼ cup unsweetened shredded coconut

4 tablespoons coriander seeds

serves 4–6

The word "greens"—used loosely to describe any leafy green—includes spring greens, Swiss chard, bok choy, beet greens, spinach, and much more. Many need only brief cooking—steam or stir-fry to retain color, nutrients, and flavor. Remove any tough stalks before cooking.

chili greens
with garlic crisps

1 lb. greens (see introduction)

2 tablespoons olive oil

4 garlic cloves, sliced

1 red serrano chile, seeded and thinly sliced

salt and freshly ground black pepper

serves 4

Coarsely chop the greens, but if using bok choy, cut lengthwise into wedges. Gently heat the olive oil in a large saucepan. Add the garlic, sauté until golden and crisp, about 2–3 minutes, then remove and set aside. Add the chile to the infused oil in the pan and cook for 1 minute.

Tip in the greens—they will splutter, so stand back. Add salt and pepper and mix well. Cover and cook, turning the greens occasionally using tongs, until tender: spring greens will take 5 minutes; Swiss chard, bok choy, and beet greens, about 3 minutes; and spinach about 1–2 minutes.

Transfer to a warmed serving dish and top with the garlic crisps to serve.

This country-style Moroccan dish is typical of regions where meat is regarded as a luxury by most families. Pulses of all kinds and, in particular, chickpeas, provide the nourishing content of these dishes. Serve with plain yogurt and warmed flatbread.

carrot and chickpea tagine
with turmeric and cilantro

Heat the oil in a tagine or heavy-based casserole dish, add the onion and garlic, and sauté until soft. Add the turmeric, cumin, cinnamon, cayenne, black pepper, honey, and carrots. Pour in enough water to cover the base of the tagine and cover with a lid. Cook gently for 10–15 minutes.

Toss in the chickpeas, check that there is still enough liquid at the base of the tagine, cover with the lid, and cook gently for a further 5–10 minutes. Season with salt, sprinkle the rosewater and cilantro leaves over the top, and serve with lemon wedges.

3–4 tablespoons olive oil

1 onion, finely chopped

3–4 garlic cloves, finely chopped

2 teaspoons ground turmeric

1–2 teaspoons cumin seeds

1 teaspoon ground cinnamon

½ teaspoon cayenne pepper

½ teaspoon ground black pepper

1 tablespoon dark honey

3–4 medium carrots, sliced on the diagonal

two 14½ oz. cans of chickpeas, drained and rinsed

1–2 tablespoons rosewater

a bunch of cilantro leaves, finely chopped

lemon wedges, to serve

sea salt

a tagine (optional)

serves 4

index

credits

photographs

KEY: ph= photographer, a=above, b=below, r=right, l=left, c=center.

Peter Cassidy
Pages 1, 2, 3, 5, 6, 8, 9bl both, 10, 13, 21, 23, 33, 35, 36, 39, 46, 47a&tc all, 49, 50, 53, 54, 57, 61, 67, 69, 70, 75, 80, 81l, 81br, 81c, 83, 99, 101, 102, 105, 117, 118, 123, 124, 125l,125b, 125r, 125cr, 127, 128, 131, 132, 135, 136,139, 149, 162, 163l, 163cl, 167, 168, 172, 175, 178, 186, 189, 192, 193 all, 195, 205, 211, 213, 217, 229, 231

William Lingwood
Pages 9ar all, 24, 27, 29, 43, 44–45, 106, 109, 110, 125a, 140, 143, 144, 152, 155, 181, 182, 214

William Reavell
Pages 81b, 81ar, 112, 115, 121, 147, 150, 163cr, 163a, 171, 191, 225

Nicki Dowey
Pages 62, 64, 84, 87, 89, 90, 196, 199

James Merrell
Endpapers, pages 40, 93, 94, 97, 200, 203, 226

Jeremy Hopley
Pages 30, 47b, 76, 79, 161, 165

Philip Webb
Pages 58, 72, 218, 221, 222, 232

Martin Brigdale
Pages 157, 163b, 185, 235

Peter Myers
Pages 17, 18, 206, 208

Ian Wallace
Pages 14, 158, 177

recipes

Ghillie Basan
Carrot and chickpea tagine with turmeric and cilantro
Spicy chicken tagine with apricots, rosemary, and ginger
Tagine of spicy kefta with lemon

Celia Brooks Brown
Charred eggplant and coconut curry
Chili greens with garlic crisps
Halloumi fajitas
Mexican gazpacho
Quesadillas
Thai coleslaw

Tamsin Burnett-Hall
Chermoula chicken with tomato pilaf
Chili beef noodles
Goan shrimp curry
Spiced salmon with chickpea dhal

Manisha Gambhir Harkins
African seafood kabobs with piri piri basting oil
Andalusian chickpea soup with chorizo, paprika, and saffron
Argentine grilled beef with chimichurri
Bulgogi
Burmese pork hinleh
Burritos with black beans and avocado salsa
Cajun-spiced chowder with corn and bacon
Chettinad chicken
Chilito
Coconut shrimp masala
Indonesian beef and coconut soup
Jerk chicken
Moroccan grilled fish with chermoula spice paste
Salsa roja
Singapore turmeric laksa
South Indian spiced rice
Spicy lamb in almond milk
Stir-fried peanut shrimp with cilantro noodles
Thai mussaman beef curry
Vegetable stir-fry with Szechuan peppercorns
Vegetarian cashew salad with tamarind dressing
Vietnamese spiced squid

Tonia George
Chicken and lentil curry with cucumber yogurt
Cumin-spiced lamb chops with chickpea mash and roasted vine tomatoes

Deep-fried eggs with rice, chile, and oyster sauce
Red curry with shrimp and pumpkin

Clare Gordon Smith
Caribbean curry
Corn crêpes with chili vegetables and tomato salsa
Shrimp brochettes with chile, papaya, and mango salsa
Spinach dhal with toasted coconut
Steamed mussels in a red chili broth
Thai seafood curry with cilantro and coconut milk
Vegetable fritters with cilantro chile mint raita

Rachael Anne Hill
Asian salmon with rice noodles
Baked sweet potatoes with Mexican beans
Chicken and chile chickpea salad
Chili scallops with spaghetti
Shrimp and butter bean rice
Shrimp and mango salad
Spicy tuna steaks with pepper noodles
Vegetable burritos

Caroline Marson
Chicken jalfrezi
Chili scallops with leeks and lime crème fraîche
Harissa-spiced chickpeas with halloumi and spinach
Indian grilled pork chops with spiced potatoes and peas
Quick Thai chicken curry
Spicy tiger shrimp salad
Stir-fried beef fajitas with guacamole and sour cream
Tom yum shrimp noodle soup

Annie Nichols
Indian dry potato curry in eggplant shells
Indian potato curry with yellow lentils
Mini potato roti with coconut and mint chutney
Tortitas de papa with chorizo and corn salsa verde

Elsa Petersen-Scheplern
Indonesian beef satays
Indonesian gado-gado
Singapore coconut laksa
Singapore pork satays
Tamarind fish laksa
Thai marinated chicken stir-fried in chili oil

Thai mee krob
Thai pork balls with chili dipping sauce
Thai spicy shrimp salad
Vietnamese chicken salad with chili-lime dressing

Louise Pickford
Chili tuna tartare pasta
Curried red lentils
Gingered chicken noodles
Oysters with spicy chorizo
Pepper 'n' spice chicken
Quick vegetarian mole
Roast five-spice chicken with ginger bok choy
Shrimp with chili oil and pistachio and mint pesto
Thai shrimp cakes with chili jam
Vietnamese pork balls

Rena Salaman
Feta and chile dip
Spicy hummus

Jennie Shapter
Chili chicken enchiladas
Indian chicken wraps with minted cucumber relish
Lamb and couscous wraps with harissa dressing
Lamb kofta wraps with minted cream
Mini spring rolls with chili dipping sauce

Fiona Smith
Crispy chili beef wontons
Egg rolls with chili tofu
Spicy crumbed squid strips

Sonia Stevenson
Capsicum chili tian with goat cheese
Chili con carne
Fish mollee
Thai green fish curry
Kerala coconut chili shrimp
Saffron and pistachio biryani
Spiced lamb with coconut

Vatcharin Bhumichitr
Chicken satay
Chicken wings with lemongrass and sweet and hot sauce
Green curry with shrimp
Pork with garlic and fresh chile
Shrimp with chile and basil
Vegetable curry
Vegetables with spicy Thai dip of young chiles

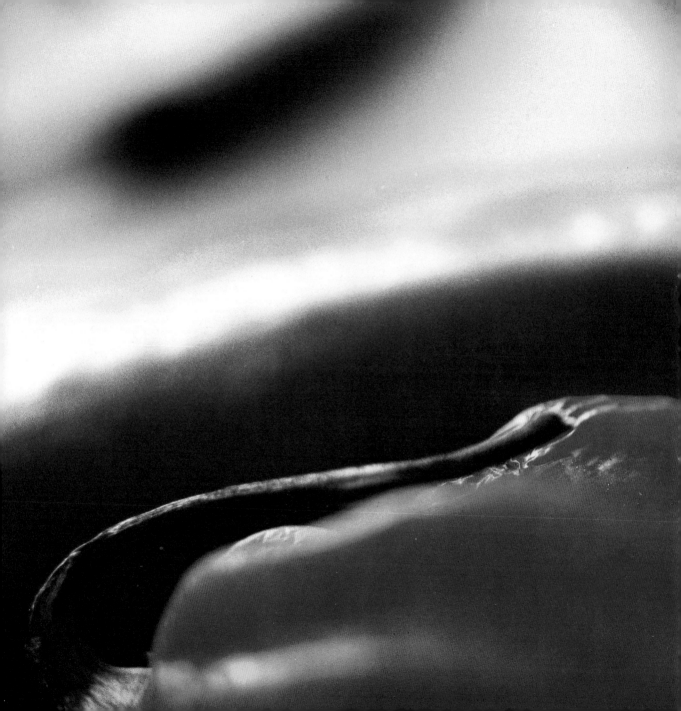